MEDIA, FEMINISM, CULTURAL STUDIES

Stepping Forward: Essays, Lectures and Interviews
by Wolfgang Iser

Wild Zones: Pornography, Art and Feminism
by Kelly Ives

Global Media Warning: Explorations of Radio, Television and the Press
by Oliver Whitehorne

'Cosmo Woman': The World of Women's Magazines
by Oliver Whitehorne

Andrea Dworkin
by Jeremy Mark Robinson

Cixous, Irigaray, Kristeva: The Jouissance of French Feminism
by Kelly Ives

Sex in Art: Pornography and Pleasure in Painting and Sculpture
by Cassidy Hughes

The Erotic Object: Sexuality in Sculpture From Prehistory to the Present Day
by Susan Quinnell

Women in Pop Music
by Helen Challis

Detonation Britain: Nuclear War in the UK
by Jeremy Mark Robinson

Julia Kristeva: Art, Love, Melancholy, Philosophy, Semiotics
by Kelly Ives

Luce Irigaray: Lips, Kissing, and the Politics of Sexual Difference
by Kelly Ives

Helene Cixous I Love You: The Jouissance of Writing
by Kelly Ives

The Poetry of Cinema
by John Madden

The Sacred Cinema of Andrei Tarkovsky
by Jeremy Mark Robinson

Disney Business, Disney Films, Disney Lands
by Daniel Cerruti

Feminism and Shakespeare
by B.D. Barnacle

Hélène Cixous

Hélène Cixous

I Love You

The *Jouissance* of Writing

Kelly Ives

CRESCENT MOON

CRESCENT MOON PUBLISHING
P.O. Box 1312, Maidstone
Kent, ME14 5XU
Great Britain
www.crmoon.com

First published 1998. Second edition 2008. Third edition 2010.
Fourth edition 2013.

Printed and bound in the U.S.A.
Set in Palatino 9 on 13pt.
Designed by Radiance Graphics.

British Library Cataloguing in Publication data

Ives, Kelly
Hélène Cixous I Love You: The Jouissance *of Writing.*
– (European Writers Series)
1. Cixous, Hélène, 1937 – Criticism and interpretation
I. Title
848.9'14'09

ISBN-13 9781861714190

CONTENTS

ABBREVIATIONS

HÉLÈNE CIXOUS

C	*The Hélène Cixous Reader*
NBW	*The Newly Born Woman*
BP	*The Book of Promethea*
EHC	"An Exchange with Hélène Cixous", interview, in V. Conley, 1991
Con	"Conversations", in S. Sellers, 1988
EF	"Extreme Fidelity", in S. Sellers,1988
DJ	"Difficult Joys", in Wilcox, 1990

JULIA KRISTEVA

K	*The Kristeva Reader*
DL	*Desire in Language*
R	*Revolution in Poetic Language*
TL	*Tales of Love*
PH	*Powers of Horror*
ACW	*About Chinese Women*
BS	*Black Sun*
SO	*Strangers to Ourselves*
QS	"A Question of Subjectivity"

LUCE IRIGARAY

I	*The Irigaray Reader*
Je	*Je, tu, nous*
S	*Speculum*
TD	*Thinking the Difference*
Sex	*This Sex Which Is Not One*

EM	"Ecce Mulier?", in P. Burgard
ML	*Marine Lover of Friedrich Nietzsche*
M	*New French Feminisms*, ed. E. Marks & I. de Courtivron
L	*Julia Kristeva*, by J. Lechte

I think about the books I will never write, that I will never read perhaps, books that are nonetheless written, are being written in the depths, books I love, it is for them that I lean out so dangerously over the edge of the abyss.

Hélène Cixous, *The Book of Promethea*

Hélène Cixous

PREFACE

This book is a poetic study of French writer and feminist Hélène Cixous. It uses sections of an earlier study of mine on the 'holy trinity' of French feminism (D. Landry, 1993, 54), namely, Hélène Cixous, Julia Kristeva and Luce Irigaray. French feminism is often reduced to meaning the writings of this holy trio, while at other times it refers to criticism in the wake of Jacques Lacan, Jacques Derrida and Michel Foucault (these three male writers are sometimes seen as an equivalent of the Cixous-Irigaray-Kristeva trinity [J. Duran, 163]). Some feminists are suspicious of calling Hélène Cixous, Luce Irigaray and Julia Kristeva 'radical': for Chris Weedon they are radical (Irigaray in particular [1987, 9]), but not for Stevi Jackson.[1] Does it matter? The works of Cixous, Irigaray and Kristeva have gone beyond such notions.

These three feminists/ philosophers/ speakers/ poets are extraordinarily enriching. Their writings are alive, and they are not limited to having one or two things to say. Rather, they say a lot, about a lot. Sometimes they write things that are outrageous, at other times they are incredibly, searingly poignant. They annoy many feminists – their insistence on the body and biology, for instance, aggravates some theorists. With its mixture of male writers (Derrida, Lacan, Foucault) and certain female writers (Kristeva, Cixous, Irigaray, Monique Wittig),

> The boundaries of 'French feminism' are thus strangely constructed: some men fall within its definition, as do women who do not call themselves feminists, but those who have always called themselves feminists are excluded.[2]

This book may irritate some people, because I do not work my way carefully and slowly through each stage of Hélène Cixous' career and *œuvre*. I do not offer in-depth analyses of every idea in Cixous' writings.

The big name cultural philosophers and critics, among whom Hélène Cixous, Luce Irigaray and Julia Kristeva are major players, publish in academic journals such as *Diacritics, Signs, Feminist Studies, Tel Quel, differences, Camera Obscura, Screen, Wide Angle, Yale French Journal, October, Social Text* and *Monthly Review*. French feminism has been made more widely available in anthologies such as the key texts *New French Feminism* (1981) and *French Feminist Thought* (1987).

French feminism is part of a movement in criticism which exalts postmodernism via modernism. The 'classic' modernists are exalted by the 'classic' postmodernists: Gustave Flaubert by Roland Barthes, René Magritte by Michel Foucault, James Joyce and Antonin Artaud by Julia Kristeva, Stéphane Mallarmé and Antonin Artaud by Derrida, Jean Genet and Marcel Proust by Hélène Cixous.[3]

Hélène Cixous was one of the most powerful of the contributors to *New French Feminisms,* most prominently in her essay "The Laugh of the Medusa", the subject of much feminist debate. Before these English anthologies appeared, however, few of the full-length works of French feminists had been translated into English. Only by about 1985 had much of the work of Cixous, Kristeva and Irigaray been translated into English (J. Duran, 177). Further, the theorists themselves (such as Monique Wittig, Annie Leclerc, Cixous, Kristeva, Irigaray), do not class themselves as 'feminists', in the same way Anglo-American feminists do.

PART ONE

FRENCH FEMINISM

1

INTRODUCTORY

HÉLÈNE CIXOUS' BIOGRAPHY

Hélène Cixous was born in Oran, Algeria, on June 5, 1937. She described her father's background as 'Sephardic - Spain - Morocco - Algeria' and her mother's as 'Ashkenazy - Austria - Hungary - Czechoslavakia (her father) and Spain (her mother)' (NBW, 131). She studied at the Université de Bordeaux, the Sorbonne, and the new, experimental post-1968 Université de Paris VIII-Vincennes, which is now at Saint Denis. Her doctoral thesis, *L'Exil de James Joyce ou l'art du remplacement* was published in 1968 (as *The Exile of James Joyce* in 1972). His first novel was *Inside* (1969). Her best known works are *The Newly Born Woman* (written with Catherine Clément) and the inspiring essay "The Laugh of the Medusa" (both 1975). In feminist theory, Cixous' most influential works have been *The Newly Born Woman*, "The Laugh of the Medusa", and "Castration or Decapitation".

By 1991, Hélène Cixous had written some 50 novels, plays, books of poetry, essays and texts (today it's 70+ works, and includes: 23 poetry books, 5 plays and 6 books of essays). She has been aligned with the French publishing house Des Femmes, and collaborated with the experimental Théâtre du Soleil (Cixous has worked for years with the theatre director Ariane Mnouchkine). Cixous' plays include *Black Sail, White Sail, Portrait of Dora, Drums On the Dam* and *The Perjured City*. In the late 1970s and 1980s, Cixous became the most frequently cited of French feminists and feminist philosophers. Following *Angst* (1977), Cixous' feminism became more militant (as with many other feminists), and was associated with the Politique et Psychoanalyse ('Psych et Po') women's political group, founded by Antoinette Fouque. Cixous felt she had reached an intellectual limit, and needed to immerse herself in the politics of relationships between women.

Late Seventies and early Eighties works were partly influenced by Martin Heidegger - his writings on language and poetics. Hélène Cixous' feminist militancy concerned itself with the problems of law, innocence, knowledge, life and death - in *Préparatifs de noces au-delà del'abîme*

(*Wedding Preparations Beyond the Abyss*, 1978), *Limonade tout était si infini* (*Lemonade All Was So Infinite*, 1982), *Illa* (1980), *With ou l'art de l'innocence* (*With or the Art of Innocence*, 1981) and *Anankè* (1979). Cixous' theory has gone into and beyond Sigmund Freud, Georg Wilhelm Hegel, Martin Heidegger, Karl Marx, Jacques Lacan, Jacques Derrida and Gilles Deleuze (V. Conley, 1991, xxii), though Derrida remains a touchstone.

Hélène Cixous' prose works of the Eighties included *La Bataille d'Arcachon* (*The Battle of Arcachon*, 1987), concerning the relations between love, presence and absence, the self and alterity; *Manne aux Mandelstams aux Mandelas* (1988) was about the Russian poet, Osip Mandelstam, who died in the Stalin era, and Nelson Mandela; *Entre l'écriture* (*Between Writing*, 1986) is a collection of writing about writing; *Jours de l'an* (*Days of the Year*, 1990) concerns notions of authorship, the relationship between the writer and writing.

Following her meeting with Anna Mnouchkine, Hélène Cixous became increasingly concerned with the theatre. Cixous' collaborations with Mnouchkine produced a series of works which looked towards 'the scene of history', as Cixous termed it. The play *L'histoire terrible ais inachevée de Norodom Sihanouk roi du Cambodge* (*The Terrible But Unfinished Story of Norodom Sihanouk, King of Cambodia*, 1984) was the result of a visit to Cambodia; *L'Indiade ou l'Inde de leurs rêves* (*The Indiad or India of Their Dreams*, 1986) concerned non-aggression, colonialism, and India's liberation; *Akhmatova* (1990) dealt with the Russian poet; the television script *La Nuit miraculeuse* (*The Miraculous Night*, 1989) was about the 1989 revolution.

The discovery of Clarice Lispector (1920-77) was pivotal for Hélène Cixous: here was a writer who seemed to be practising an *écriture féminine*, who was exploring the very territory Cixous wished to investigate. Instead of sinking down into the tragic, masculine, Kafkan worldview, Cixous prefers the positive view of Lispector, who says that 'to live is sufficient. I need nothing else but to live; living produces living. She does not say, "not not", she says the opposite. She affirms life in a pure affirmation; that is "feminine", that is the source itself' (EHC, 154).

Lispector emphasized what has become one of Cixous' key themes (as with André Gide, Anaïs Nin and Samuel Beckett): the relationship between life and writing. Lispector emphasized the flow of language, which Cixous characterized as the 'arrival in language': 'What flows has already traversed me, blood and milk, urine and tears. I flow, am being flown without ever dying' (*Portrait du soleil*, 54). Chantal Chawaf also wrote of the physical fluidity of women's writing: 'I feel the political fecundity of mucus, milk, sperm, secretions which gush out to liberate energies and give them back to the world' (in M, 178).

Hélène Cixous has had a number of books written about her work: Verena Andermatt Conley has published one of the best studies (in two editions, 1984 and 1990); Claudine Fisher's *La Cosmogonie d'Hélène Cixous* (1988) is a meticulous study of Cixous' work; collections of writings on Cixous include a *Boundary* special issue (1984), conference proceedings such as *The Body and the Text* (1991), and *Hélène Cixous, chemins d'une écriture*; other important critics of Cixous include Toril Moi, Françoise van Rossum-Guyon, Morag Shiach, Alice Jardine, Susan Sellers, Donna Stanton and Vivian Kogan. *The Hélène Cixous Reader* is a superb collection of her writings, with one of the most cogent explications of her texts by Susan Sellers.

Some critics have upbraided Mme Cixous for her apparent essentialism (Toril Moi, Elaine Showalter), while others have sought to present a more sympathetic (or non-essentialist) reading of her work (Morag Shiach, Christiane Makward, Claudine Fisher, Verena Conley, Helen Wilcox).[1]

The American feminist Camille Paglia claimed to have 'swept Hélène Cixous into the dustbin of history'. Paglia regarded the French feminists – Cixous, Irigaray and Kristeva and their postmodern, deconstructionist philosophy – as 'sloppy, third-rate thinkers' (1995, 348, 501). Paglia swiped at 'that damp sob sister, Hélène Cixous, with her diarrhoea prose', and 'Irigaray, the pompous lap dog of Parisian café despots doing her grim, sledge-hammer elephant walk through small points' (1992, 243-4). you gotta love Paglia! Gayatri Chakravorty Spivak is also critical of Cixous' poetics, the way in which Cixous equates the literary *avant garde* with political radicalism (in "French feminism in an international frame").

Of the three French feminists cited as a trinity, Hélène Cixous has perhaps been the most influential, or at least the most widely cited by critics and writers. Cixous is referred to in all manner of places.

Here are a few: a *Screen* article by Mary Ann Doane ("Film and the Masquerade" [J. Caughie, 1992]); Hélène Cixous is cited in an essay on lesbian cinema, discussing lesbian identity; Anne Wales cites Cixous' theory of female difference in "The Laugh of the Medusa" in an essay on *Desperately Seeking Susan*; Jean Andrews refers to Cixous' *The Newly Born Woman* in a piece on the opera *Carmen*; Marilyn Farwell's excellent *Heterosexual Plots and Lesbian Narratives* (1996) brings Cixous into an analysis of lesbian difference; in their book on *Female Fetishism*, Lorraine Gamman and Merja Makinen (1994) discuss the trio of French feminists; Cixous' concept of woman as 'Other' (in, again, "The Laugh of the Medusa"), is discussed in an essay on mediæval poetry by St. John E. Flynn; Kadiatu Kanneh relates Cixous' theories of the dark, unconscious, fluid feminine to issues of race, gender and sexuality (in I. Armstrong, 1992); Cixous' sense of bisexuality in "Sorties" is cited in Clare Hemmings' essay on sexual identity; in Cath Stowers's piece on Jeanette Winterson's fiction, Cixous' *l'écriture féminine*, "Sorties" and sense of difference are explored; in *(Un)like Subjects* Geraldine Meaney related Cixous' concepts of castration and the Medusa to modern women's fiction (1993); Linda Ruth Williams refers to Cixous' view of the mother in her study of psychoanalysis and literature (1995); Gregory Woods cites Cixous' theory of libidinal economy in a discussion of Ernest Hemingway's sexual politics (in J. Still, 1993); Howard Eilberg-Schwartz explored the relation between castration, beheading, language, expression and the feminine, *pace* Cixous and Sigmund Freud (1995, 6f); Philip Cox used Cixous' theories of feminine culture (in "Sorties" and "Castration or Decapitation") in his study of British Romantic poets; in an essay on Cixous, Mikhail Bakhtin and women's writing, Lisa Gasbarrone takes "The Laugh of the Medusa" as her starting-point (in K. Hohne, 1994); Ros

Ballaster cited Cixous' 1976 essay on Freud in a survey of Gothic fiction and feminism; there have been important essays on the relation between Cixous and Friedrich Nietzsche (in P. Burgard, 1994); Ib Johansen's "The Semiotics of Laughter" inevitably refers to "The Laugh of the Medusa" and "Castration or Decapitation" (in F. Barker, 1996); many surveys, guidebooks and encyclopædias have chapters or sections either on Cixous or French feminism (such as S. Mills, 1996; M. Humm, 1992; J. Still and Worton, 1993; T. Moi, 1985; and Ann Rosalind Jones's chapter in *The New Feminist Criticism* [E. Showalter, 1986]).[1]

Hélène Cixous, Luce Irigaray and Julia Kristeva all have different modes of writing. There are times when they are writing in the sober, measured tones of a cultural critic, philosopher or psychoanalyst (Cixous much prefers to consider herself a poet rather than a philosopher). They have strident feminist voices (Cixous and Irigaray more than Kristeva). They have personal reminiscence modes. They have a relaxed, informal mode in interviews. And, most powerful of all, they have lyrical modes. Thus, Cixous, the most 'poetic' of the three, will break into a visionary, ultra-lyrical way of writing. Cixous' aim is for a language that is poetic, that is 'sufficiently transparent, sufficiently supple, intense, faithful' and musical so that there would be reparation not separation (EHC, 146).

Hélène Cixous says she has four or five modes of writing, which include essays, criticism, theatre, poetic fiction and her private notebooks which she writes 'only to myself and which no one will ever read, where I exercise a different style'. No single form of writing is valued above the others, Cixous says; each one 'has a particular urgency, an individual force, a necessity' ("Preface", C, xvi). Cixous' fictions are not novels in the traditional sense; they break laws, they are free-form and move outside of literary genres. She invents words, puns, deliberately alters grammar and spelling. 'Cixous writes with an erotic, fluid syntax and new images, puns and absences in order to release women's bodies from existing representations', Maggie Humm remarked of "The Laugh of the Medusa" (1992, 194). For Cixous, poetry should be socially transformative, dense, mysterious, intense, subverting everyday clichés (V. Conley, 1991, 5).

In "Stabat Mater", Julia Kristeva wrote passionately of her experience of childbirth:

> Nights of wakefulness, scattered sleep, sweetness of the child, warm mercury in my arms, cajolery, affection, defenceless body, his or mine, sheltered, protected. A wave swells again, when he goes to sleep, under my skin – tummy, thighs, legs: sleep of the muscles, not of the brain, sleep of the flesh. The wakeful tongue quietly remembers another withdrawal, mine: a blossoming heaviness in the middle of the bed, of a hollow, of the sea... (K, 171-2)

Luce Irigaray, too, changes – though less frequently than Hélène Cixous – from a critical to a lyrical form. Thus, in a piece such as "When Our Lips Speak Together", Irigaray will write poetic sentences such as '[k]iss me. Two lips kiss two lips, and openness is ours again.' This is the kind of phrase which never appears in most cultural theorists outside of quotation marks. One doesn't find Jacques Derrida, Jacques Lacan, Gilles Deleuze, Jean Baudrillard, Jean François Lyotard, Mikhail Bakhtin, Michel Foucault, Louis Althusser, Fredric Jameson, Roland Barthes or Jean-Paul Sartre writing 'kiss me' very often. Well, perhaps Foucault and Barthes said 'kiss me' in darkened hotel rooms – but not in scholarly books published by Minuit or Gallimard.

What marks Hélène Cixous, Luce Irigaray and Julia Kristeva apart from many cultural theorists and philosophers, then, is this personal, confessional and poetic way of writing, where they directly address the reader as the other, the 'you' in an intimate relationship. Jacques Derrida, Michel Foucault, Jean Baudrillard, Michel de Certeau, Terry Eagleton and Ramon Jakobson are rarely, if ever, this personal. Cixous, Irigaray and Kristeva, then, are more than simply cultural critics, shuffling between the café and the university library, lighting their pipes (Freud) or chain-smoking cigarettes (Sartre), or bitching about America (any French intellectual), while they ponder on imponderables, chat about prostitutes and brothels with their cronies and write up the occasional philosophical paper.

Hélène Cixous, Luce Irigaray and Julia Kristeva are considerable poets as well as psychoanalysts and philosophers. Their writings have a tremendous *verve*, even when they are dealing with the arid heights of abstruse semiological theory. Kristeva, for example, in writing of childbirth in "Stabat Mater", foregrounds her own experience in ways which many masculinist cultural critics do not, would not, or could not. Kristeva very deliberately places her own experience of something very much in the province of 'women's experience' in a cultural theory essay.

Of course, masculinist critics and writers have oft discussed sex, violence and death from 'first hand' experience, so to speak (Marquis de Sade, Georges Bataille, Jean-Paul Sartre and Michel Foucault), but for Julia Kristeva the experience of motherhood decentres men and masculinist theory. Feminist theorists and poets such as Hélène Cixous, Luce Irigaray and Julia Kristeva are valuable, then, precisely because they foreground experiences that have been sidelined or stereotyped for centuries. Kristeva's account of childbirth knocks away conventional accounts, such as from traditional science and medicine, or from the early Christian 'fathers', such as St Augustine, who maintained, in the bizarre way of his, that people are all born between fæces and urine. The French feminists counter this demonization of female sexuality and make it a central part of their study. The effect of such foregrounding of female sexuality is disruptive and subversive. As Luce Irigaray said in *This Sex Which Is Not One*: 'what is most strictly forbidden to women today is that they should attempt to express their own pleasure' (I, 125).

Experience itself is not to be sidelined, as Elizabeth Grosz has suggested in *Volatile Bodies*, but is a useful issue in feminism: Grosz has drawn on the philosophy of Maurice Merleau-Ponty in this regard. However, experience is also culturally conditioned:

> Experience is not outside social, political, historical, and cultural forces and in this sense cannot provide an outside vantage point from which to judge them. Merleau-Ponty's understanding of the constructed, synthetic nature of experience, its simultaneously active and passive functioning, its role in both the inscription and subversion of socio-

political values, provides a crucial confirmation of many feminists' unspoken assumptions regarding women's experiences. (94-95)

Hélène Cixous, Luce Irigaray and Julia Kristeva pull language apart and remake it. They often put words in parentheses and quotes, or split them up, or hyphenate them. Word plays such as 'specula(riza)tion' are common in their work. Cixous' word-games include this sentence from *Portrait du Soleil*: '*et maintenant de quel sang signer ça?*' Cixous plays on *sang* (blood) and *sans* (without, in/ out), *s(a)igner* (to bleed and to sign), *ça* (it/ id), *sa* (signifier, from Georg Wilhelm Hegel's SA - *savoir absolut*). In *Neutre* Cixous plays with Samson and *sans, sans* (separating himself from himself), *sans sang* (without blood), *sans son* (without sound or voice), *son son* (sound sound), *cent sangs* (hundred bloods), *cent cent* (hundred hundred). In *Prénoms de personne* Cixous plays with the phrase *me délie et me délit*, which can be translated as 'seduces and unbinds me', 'to take out of the bed' or 'to unbind and to unread from the known'. The phrases *me délie* and *me délit* allude to Maurice Scève's Renaissance poem cycle *Délie*; *délit*, 'the crime dividing the idea'; and to word games such as the feminine *idée* and the masculine *délit*; *el(le)*, *il*; *l'i* and the letter 'i' (V. Conley, 1991, 19). If the masculine is evoked in Cixous' texts, so is the feminine: 'he' plus 'she', *un il* ('a he') plus *un île* ('a he-she') and *un el* ('a she-he') (in *Déluge* and *La*). There is 'the man who is your mother' (in *Angst*) and 'the son who is a daughter' (in *La*). The mute 'e' in the French 'feminine' is deployed: *enfante* ('she-child), *fauconne* ('female falcon'), *ciel/le ciel bleue* ('feminine sky', 'feminine blue'), *la frère* ('she-brother') and *en soi* ('herself-inner-self').

Hélène Cixous, Luce Irigaray and Julia Kristeva parody classic texts and draw attention to hypocrisy and banality. They snuggle up close to classic philosophic texts and parody them in order to bring out the blind spots, repressions and hypocrisies. Irigaray uses mimicry and pastiche to interrogate philosophy; she has rewritten Friedrich Nietzsche and Sigmund Freud, much as Monique Wittig has reworked Dante Alighieri and Miguel Cervantes, and Cixous has tackled Greek mythology, Freud and the *Bible*.

In particular, words such as *il* and *elle,* the gendering of French words, is central to their reworking of language and philosophy. This makes their writing particularly difficult to translate, because they are moving back and forth, continually, between received and ironic/ polemical treatments of language. Thus, translators and editors are forced to interject, and set words in square brackets [thus], in order to remind the reader of the original French text.

Hélène Cixous and Luce Irigaray are the most playful in this respect: for this reason, their texts should always, ideally, be quoted in the French and in translation. However, as this is a study written in English, I have not assumed that readers can read French, so I have generally drawn on the English translations of Cixous, Irigaray and Kristeva that are available. Where possible, I have used the collections of writings or anthologies of Cixous, Irigaray and Kristeva (*The Hélène Cixous Reader* [Routledge], *The Irigaray Reader* [Blackwell] and *The Kristeva Reader* [Blackwell]), as these are generally available. These are scholarly, well-edited selections of key works of Cixous, Irigaray and Kristeva. Unfortunately, many of the English translations of Cixous, Irigaray and Kristeva are published in less widely available editions (by University of Minnesota Press, Columbia University Press, Harvard University Press, Athlone Press and Cornell University Press). These are excellent editions, but Cixous, Irigaray and Kristeva have not been taken up by a mainstream publisher – their works remain available only in large or specialist stores.

French writers are especially prone to word games (and critics sometimes try to ape them, desperate to show off). The trouble with word games and puns is that they often come across as immature, ponpous, and kinda pointless. Showy, self-conscious. 'Look at me! Look what I can do with L-Ah-nN^^Nn<>//*Goo* – u[1234567890]-A-g-e.'

2

FRENCH FEMINIST POETICS: THE ISSUES OF FEMINIST AND WOMEN'S ART

FEMALE SEXUALITY

One of the problems that feminists have addressed with regard to women's art is: can there be a truly 'female' or 'feminine' or 'women's' art? Is art made by women (women's art) ever completely free of patriarchal influences, structures, forms? Can there be a women's art that exists in its own female space, away from patriarchy and masculinist ideas and experiences? Julia Kristeva is pessimistic on this contentious issue. For her, there has been no 'female writing' thus far in our culture. She said in 1977:

> If we confine ourselves to the *radical* nature of what is today called 'writing', that is, if we submit meaning and the speaking subject in language to a radical examination and then reconstitute them in a more polyvalent than fragile manner, there is nothing in either past or recent publications by women that permits us to claim that a specifically female writing exists.[1]

The feminist critical view of modernist æsthetics is that it is biased towards masculinism; the French feminists, such as Julia Kristeva and Hélène Cixous, have realigned modernism towards feminist æsthetics and the notion of *écriture féminine*. The emphasis in *écriture féminine* on fluidity, fragmentation, indeterminacy and multiple viewpoints undermines the masculinist monolithic nature of literary modernism. The modernist text is 'said to be anti-patriarchal, feminine and radical'.[2]

Most writing is masculine, Hélène Cixous says, and women are thus doing 'someone else's – man's – writing, and in their innocence sustain it and give it voice' ("Le Sexe ou la tête?", 52). In French feminism the text is primary, and a text can be feminine' regardless of who creates it. For Cixous a man can write a 'feminine text (such as Marcel Proust or Jean Genet). Cixous' book *La Jeune Née* plays with name Jean Genet.

The most complete example of 'feminine writing', in Hélène Cixous' view, is that of Clarice Lispector (in "At Hélène Cixous Pleasure", C, xxx). For Cixous, 'feminine writing' does not need to construct a masculine self, in order to feel dominant; instead, alternative relations and expressions are created. *Écriture féminine* may thus be revolutionary, because it initiates social and political changes. *Écriture féminine,* Cixous says, in *The Newly Borm Woman,* may not be obliged to reproduce the system of 'vileness and compromise'; it may escape the 'infernal repetition', to a place 'where *it* writes itself, where *it* dreams, where invents new worlds' (72). For Cixous, pleasure, *jouissance,* it disrupts capitalism. It disorders society.

Critics have asked of Hélène Cixous' notion of *écriture féminine,* how important is it that writers of *écriture féminine,* such as Jean Genet and Marcel Proust, were homosexual? Or as Gregory Woods put it, [i]s what is *féminine* about their *écriture* related to the fact that they liked being fucked by men?'[3] That is, there may be a homophobic component in the assumed link between femininity and homosexuality.

Hélène Cixous' evocation of *écriture féminine* may conceal a 'blithe heterosexism' which unconsciously privileges heterosexual above homosexual male writing (ib., 149). In "Sorties", where Cixous provides a list of oppositions, the ones on the 'night' or 'feminine' side are the ones most often associated with poetry: 'mother', 'heart', 'sensitive', 'moon', 'night', and 'nature' (M, 90).

For Hélène Cixous, most writing, by men or women, is masculine. She writes:

> Most women are like this; they do someone else's – man's – writing, and in their innocence sustain it and give it voice, and end up producing writing that's in effect masculine.[4]

The notion of '*écriture féminine*' of Luce Irigaray and Hélène Cixous, which's much discussed in feminist literary criticism,[5] is rejected by Monique Wittig. Wittig also rejects the notions of 'man' and 'woman'. For her, 'woman' is a historical, political, ideological and cultural construct. She writes that "woman' has meaning only in heterosexual systems of thought and heterosexual economic systems'.[6]

The discussion of women's art and women artists is, many feminists feel, crucial to feminism. After all, *one knows what male artists are like,* and one is utterly familiar with male art. One is surrounded, embedded, drenched, choked, smothered by patriarchal art and culture, by male-orientated culture (even if not specifically male-*made* culture). Male projections, often onto women, have become dogma. Masculinist fears of the body, and sexuality, have been projected onto women, so that the vagina becomes a hell hole, the 'gateway to Hell'. As Luce Irigaray writes: men's '*fantasies lay down the law*'.[7]

> God is the name [writes Hélène Cixous] of the law, the name of punishment, of the masculine figure who cannot let himself act in a way that would make people stop at a stage of *jouissance*, of pleasure, simply because otherwise there would be no society, no capitalism, no power struggle; there would not be that which has become our civilization; all this is completely banal. (EHC, 145)

Who is 'woman'? Hélène Cixous asks in *The Newly Born Woman*, and answers, in her fervent, utopian mode, that woman's 'libido is cosmic, just as her unconsciousness is worldwide'; she

> goes on and on infinitely. She alone cares and wants to know from within where she, the one excluded, has never ceased to hear what-comes-before-language reverberating... She refuses life nothing... she surprises herself at seeing, being, pleasuring in her gift of changeability. I am spacious singing Flesh: onto which is grafted no one knows which I – which masculine or feminine, more or less human but above all living, because changing I. (88; C, 44-45)

In a patriarchal culture, male art is seen as the hegemony which (female) feminists have to subvert. For too long, some feminists claim, women's art has been defined as simply 'not male'/ 'men's art'. It is defined by its non-inclusion in the traditional sphere of men's/ male/ masculine art. As Luce Irigaray puts it: '[b]eing a woman is equated with not being a man' (Je, 71).

There are many feminists who advocate the exaltation of all manner of women artists, who argue for a 'women's art' based on women artists, who want people to look at women artists. There are other feminists who deny the primacy of the author, who say that the work - the text - is primary, who deny the transparency of the text (this is one of Julia Kristeva's projects).

Toril Moi and many other feminist critics have questioned the humanist notion of 'realism' or 'authenticity', where a text is seen to reflect the actual experience of the one who created it. Humanist criticism sees a direct relation between author and text, assuming that the artwork is a direct expression of the artist's experience. Artists, however, know that very often the artwork ends up being far away from what they intended to express or communicate. Texts do not simply reflect directly the author's perception of life. The only assessment of a text would be how well the author has perceived the 'real world'. These approaches ignore how complex textual production is, with its many literary and non-literary influences, including the social, political, institutional and psychological (T. Moi, 1985, 45).

HÉLÈNE CIXOUS' POETICS

And the mystery is that we confuse invent and believe. We invent this word Death and the word becomes our master, and do we not disinvent? One word, and here we are crippled, cold, off course, and for years... And what an ugly word: "Death." Die for a word? At least let it be magical, and ring at God's door, like the word "Absinth," or the word "Mystical." At least a quicksilver horse, or the star with the singing horses.

Hélène Cixous, *First Days of the Year* (C, 185-6)

Hélène Cixous is as idealistic and visionary in her writings on love as Luce Irigaray. She describes love as a combination of life *and* art, speaking in terms of experience *and* writing, of caresses *and* poetry, of emotion *and* its evocation in language. In *To Live the Orange* the narrator dedicates the three aspects of love to her peers:

> To all of my amies for whom loving the moment is a necessity, saving the moment is such a difficult thing, and we never have the necessary time, the slow, sanguineous time, that is the condition of this love, the pensive, tranquil time that has the courage to let last, I dedicate the three gifts: slowness which is the essence of tenderness; a cup of passion-fruits whose flesh presents in its heart filaments comparable to the styles that poetry bears; and the *spelaïon*, as it is in itself a gourd full of voices, an enchanted ear, the instrument of a continuous music, an open, bottomless species of orange. (C, 88)

In this sort of cosmic, poetic writing, Hélène Cixous is spectacular. But one has to buy it all, all at once. It is a writing of flow and mood: to stop and analyze it oddly destroys its magic: one sees how silly many of the wild statements are. 'The orange is a beginning', for example: what does that *mean*?

"The Laugh of the Medusa" is a celebration of women's culture. Not so much an analysis as a 'sustained exhortation' (G. Meaney, 15). Even if feminist critics could not endorse the views Hélène Cixous puts forward in "The Laugh of the Medusa", which some perceive as essentialist, they could at least admire the wild abandon of the writing in it (ib., 58). Cixous' Medusa tract reclaims the negative power that men have projected onto women (the castrating Medusa's stare). The Medusa head is rejoined to the body which writes. 'More body, hence more writing'. In writing, Cixous says in *The Newly Born Woman,* women could re-instate their relationship with their sexuality, their organs, their pleasures, their forces, their goods' (NBW, 97). 'Write yourself: your body must make itself heard', she says (ib.). Women are alienated from their bodies, Cixous asserts, so their bodies are Africa, a dark continent, something fearful, so women's 'sex still frightens them. Their bodies, which they haven't dared enjoy, have been colonized. Woman is disgusted by woman and fears her' (NBW, 68).

Hélène Cixous enthuses in "The Laugh of the Medusa":

> Text: my body - shot through with streams of song; I don't mean the overbearing, clutchy "mother" but, rather, what touches you, the equivoice that affects you, fills you breast with an urge to come to language and launches your force; the rhythm that laughs you; the intimate recipient who makes all metaphors possible and desire... (M, 252)

For Hélène Cixous, experience is the teacher. 'I think that we traverse in time moments which, little by little, allow us to advance and to learn to live.' In her case, Cixous sees herself as someone who will never be at peace, will never stop learning, because she is 'really a questioner'. 'Simply, the things I do not understand renew themselves incessantly' (EHC, 161). While everything has to be re-learnt, there are certain fundamental truths in life. There 'is truth' Cixous says, and 'it's the same everywhere... Life has its secrets and they are always the same, but they have to be rediscovered. Truth has to be worked for' (Con, 143). Cixous is much concerned with time, patience and waiting, and how waiting relates to the present moment, living in the moment. The old kind of time, the 'human time', has been supplanted in modern, urban life by a speeded-up time, a time accelerated by modern technologies and television. 'As soon as one is in an urban space, one does not have time anymore. Time flies by us, we do not live it. One must leave and retreat', Cixous said (EHC, 160-1). Cixous does not advocate a resigned kind of patience, a Christian patience, nor a waiting imposed by cruelty or violence, imposed by outside forces; but

> a wait that is capable of taking pleasure in each instant, that does not jump over instants by saying, I cannot wait until the end of nine months. She enjoys each time, each measure. Clarice Lispector, for example, sings the present, so that each moment, each instant, is a blessing lived to its fullest. (EHC, 160)

It is crucial to make art, to write, to create, as every feminist, of whatever political belief, agrees. One must write, because otherwise one gets written. If one doesn't write, someone else will 'write' you. One'll be written over, written out, edited, selected, controlled, censored, cut up, packaged, suffocated. All feminists agree that, whatever one believes, and whatever one desires, whether emotionally, politically, or socially, writing and creating are absolutely essential. Cixous asserts: 'I will say this: today, writing is for women' (NBW, 158).

Hélène Cixous says, in the famous article "The Laugh of the Medusa", '[a]nd why don't you write? Write! Writing is for you, you are for you... Write, let no one hold you back, let nothing stop you' (M, 246-7). For Cixous (who is loved and loathed by feminists nearly as energetically as Andrea Dworkin or Germaine Greer or Princess Diana), writing is absolutely crucial, and central. Cixous asserted that 'writing, writing poetically, treating language as one of the most important things in the world, today sounds mad. Yet for human beings it is the first most important thing' (DJ, 23). Writing is oxygen to her, she must write to live, as she says:

> Having never been without writing, having writing in my body, at my throat, on my lips... to me my texts are elements of a whole which interweaves my own story. ("Preface", C, xv)

You can 'read' creatively, if you don't write. Much of feminist theory is based on 'reading' texts as a woman, a feminist, a lesbian. If the author is 'dead', and the text is primary, then deeply engaging with texts is crucial. Hence the importance, too, of feminist æsthetic and philosophic criticism, which aims to interpret all manner of texts. '

> I believe in what we call in French *quand même*, the however, the nevertheless, or the still, because there are readers, because there are writers. For me joy is always linked to the possibility of sharing in a work of art. (DJ, 25)

The reader, at least, is 'real'. The reader, it would seem, is truly flesh and blood, not a linguistic abstraction. Even here, though, some feminists dispute the 'reality' or 'authenticity' of the body; for the body, like education or desire or the family, is culturally and socially conditioned. That is, there is no such thing as a 'pure' reality, a 'pure' experience, a 'pure' response to a text, a response that is not modulated by all manner of social, societal, familial, psychological, political, ideological and cultural influences. In feminism, the scenario is not simply a woman and a book, existing completely separately from everything else, in some utopian place. No, there is so much that gets in the way of the seemingly 'innocent' or 'pure' exchange between a woman and an artwork, a person and a text. But the personal response is crucial, and alive. Reading can be, in itself, radical and transformative.

For Elizabeth Grosz, the body isn't simply a natural or organic thing or process; there is always a lot more going on with the body – to do with the cultural, social and psychological impact on it, as she explains in her stunning book *Volatile Bodies*:

> What psychoanalytic theory makes clear is that the body is literally written on, inscribed, by desire and signification, at the anatomical, physiological, and neurological levels. The body is in sense naturally or innately psychical, sexual, or sexed. It is indeterminate and indeterminable outside its social constitution as a body of a particular type. This implies that the body which it presumes and helps to explain is an open-ended, pliable set of significations, capable of being rewritten, reconstituted, in quite other terms than those which mark it, and consequently capable of reinscribing the forms of sexed identity and psychical subjectivity at work today. (60-61)

As Grosz reminds us, human beings always live in their bodies: they always have a body. They can't remain human without a body:

> Human subjects never simply *have* a body; rather, the body is always necessarily the object and subject of attitudes and judgements. It is psychically invested, never a matter of indifference. Human being love their bodies (or, what amounts libidinally to the same thing, they hate them or parts of them). The body never has merely instrumental or utilitarian value for the subject. (ib., 81)

Even when it is nude, the body exhibits traces of its culture, its society, its politics, its use, and its practices, as Grosz notes:

> The naked European/ American/ African/ Asian/ Australian body (and clearly even within these categories there is enormous cultural variation) is still marked by its disciplinary history, by its habitual patterns of movement, by the corporeal commitments it has undertaken in day-to-day life. It is in no sense a natural body, for it is as culturally, racially, sexually, possibly even as class distinctive, as it would be it if were clothed.

In the advanced capitalist, technological world, the body is not a 'natural' form any more, as Elizabeth Grosz explains in *Volatile Bodies*: clothing, exercise, jewellery, lifestyle, habits, negotiations of the cultural and social as well as the physical environment, and all sorts of activities alter it, inscribe it, turn it into something definitely not 'natural':

> Makeup, stilettos, bras, hair sprays, clothing, underclothing mark women's bodies, whether black or white, in ways in which hair styles, professional training, personal grooming, gait, posture, body building, and sports may mark men's. There is nothing natural or ahistorical about these modes of corporeal inscriptions. Through then, bodies are make amenable to the prevailing exigencies of power. They make the flesh into a particular type of body – pagan, primitive, medieval, capitalist, Italian, American, Australian. (142)

Hélène Cixous is a dreamer. 'I also know that everything that occurs in dreams can occur in reality. Because we only dream true' (*Manna to the Mandelstams to the Mandelas*, C, 166). She acknowledges the immense importance of dreams for her. 'I owe everything, almost everything to dream', she admits (EHC, 154). Dreams are 'the deepest, the most essential life', and are crucial in the creative enterprise: one must always keep connected to the dream life of the unconscious (EHC, 154-5). If one becomes alienated or cut off from the dream life, it is

> a betrayal of the deepest elements in one's relationship with the uncon-

> scious. The unconscious, as we know it, does not lie. So when I cannot write, that means that I am lying in my inner depth. (EHC, 155)

Hélène Cixous reckons people should write as they dream because in their dreams they don't lie:

> we should try and write as our dreams teach us; shamelessly, fearlessly, and by facing what is inside every human being – sheer violence, disgust, terror, shit, invention, poetry. Our dreams are the greater poets. (DJ, 22)

Hélène Cixous writes at a running pace; a work is started in the middle ('[w]e are in the middle', she writes in *L'Ange au secret*, 11). Works are already begun, already in process, but the subject is never certain. Cixous says it's a mystery to her what she writes about when she sits down to write: '[i]t's a mystery; there where it grabs, where it bursts forth, where it gathers like rain' (interview, in C, 208). Mireille Calle Gruber calls Cixous 'the goddess of recollection, of difference, of multiplication' (C, 213).

> I write – yet I am not unaware of it: everything that is written runs out of silence and everything is written running out of breath [Cixous writes]. But silence is not lost; it is kept to one side. But I am not unaware: writing is not an end. I think: I do not write to write, I write to read better: I write a more subtle body than my busy body, the tympan body, I write – I think – ears that are more refined than my ears, that only hear what makes noise, but do not hear what moves, works, speaks, exit incessantly without being noticed, without boasting. I write, have written, to slow down, to approach immersed in writing where everything can listen to everything else infinitely more slowly. (*(With) Or the Art of Innocence*, C, 98)
> I am raining. My wetness is passionate. I foam. The seas are all on edge… I rain down thousands of words that never sipped air before. (*Le Livre de Promethea*, 77)

And in *The Newly Born Woman* Hélène Cixous and Catherine Clément write that '[w]riting is working; being worked; questioning (in) the between (letting oneself be questioned) of same *and of* other without which nothing lives' (86; C, 43).

In her essay "Castration or Decapitation", Hélène Cixous offered a counter-point to Freudian psychoanalysis's theory of castration. If men suffered from castration anxiety, Cixous suggested, then women suffered from decapitation anxiety. That is, women could only keep their heads 'on the condition that they lose them, lose them, that is, to complete silence, turned into automatons' (1981). Cixous reversed psychoanalysis's emphasis on male sexuality and psychology; women, in Cixous' view, were not passively accepting their gender identity, but were 'actively responding to the threat of losing their heads' (H. Eilberg-Schwartz, 7). Typically for Cixous, her decapitation anxiety is related directly to female expression. Instead of female decapitation being seen, in Sigmund Freud's model of castration anxiety, as a symbol of male castration anxiety, female decapitation results from male castration anxiety. Cixous' theory of female decapitation revises Freud's Medusa theory. For Cixous, male castration is really about men losing their power, which she reads as mainly their power over women. When men are anxious about their manhood and power, Cixous suggests, they try to deny women their identity and language.

FRIEDRICH NIETZSCHE AND FRENCH FEMINISM

Friedrich Nietzsche (1844-1900) has been one of the major philosophic encounters in the work of Luce Irigaray, and to a lesser extent in in the work of Hélène Cixous and Julia Kristeva. Recent feminist analyses of Nietzsche have gone far beyond the stereotype of Nietzsche as a misogynist: his relation to the 'feminine', to 'woman' and 'women', is much more complicated than mere woman-hating and sexism.[1]

Every intellectual and writer seems to have to grapple with Friedrich

Nietzsche as some time or other (especially the French philosophers: Georges Bataille, Hélène Cixous, Sarah Kofman, Gilles Deleuze, Jacques Derrida and Jean-Paul Sartre). For Derrida, Nietzsche's relationship with the feminine was embodied by his identification with three types of women: the castrating woman, the castrated woman, and the affirming woman. 'Nietzsche was all these', wrote Derrida - sometimes at once, successively or simultaneously.[2] For some feminist critics, the figure behind these masks may be Nietzsche's mother, and his ambiguous relationship with his mother may inform some of his ambivalent attitudes towards women.[3]

The influence of Lou Andreas-Salomé (1861-1937) on Friedrich Nietzsche has been noted by some feminist critics, including French feminist Sarah Kofman. Nietzsche was besotted with Andreas-Salomé, calling her 'sharp-sighted as an eagle and courageous as a lion'.[4] Andreas-Salomé was the only erotic/ philosophic focus in Nietzsche's otherwise celibate experience of women.[5] Kofman has wondered whether Andreas-Salomé was a model for that narcissistic woman which men love, the type that demands to be loved. Kofman considers this narcissistic woman in relation to Nietzsche, and wonders whether Andreas-Salomé was the mediator of the theory of narcissism between Nietzsche and Sigmund Freud.[6] Andreas-Salomé's notion of the narcissistic woman, and her thoughts on the artist, influenced Nietzsche.

In the Nietzschean-Andreas-Saloméan view, the (male) artist, if he is lucky, can aspire to the creativity of the woman, to become a 'birther' (*Gebärerin*), which may make him 'more whole, more organic, fused... with what he creates, just as woman is,' Andreas-Salomé wrote in her 1899 essay "Die in such ruhende Frau": 'and maintains him as it were in a joy of spiritual pregnancy, which lives deep within itself.'[7] Luce Irigaray was sceptical of such a project. Other critics have analyzed Cixous' reading of Nietzsche.[8]

Julia Kristeva's relation to Friedrich Nietzsche has been less important than in Hélène Cixous and Luce Irigaray. Jacques Lacan and Sigmund Freud figure much larger in Kristeva's theory than Nietzsche. Kristeva is sceptical of Nietzsche's philosophy in *About Chinese Women*, when she writes: 'Nietzsche would not have known how to be a woman. A woman has nothing to laugh about when the symbolic order collapses' (K, 150). Even so, some critics have seen similarities between the philosophies of Kristeva and Nietzsche, between the notion of rebirth (in Kristeva's interpretation of melancholy and Nietzsche's revaluation of values).[9] Nietzsche's relation to the maternal is more in tune with Kristeva's poetics. Nietzsche's problem was that he conflated 'woman', the 'feminine' and motherhood: in his works, woman becomes 'the fetish of eternal pregnancy', a phallic mother of eternal potency: sexually, she is feared, but as a mother she is exalted.[10] For Sigmund Freud, the fetish was a substitute for the missing penis of the mother, a view that perpetuated the fantasy of the phallic mother; Nietzsche fetishized the womb and women's (spiritual) fecundity. He spoke in Goddess-oriented terms, the kind familiar from thousands of years of mythology and poetry, of the 'eternally creative primordial mother'.[11]

✤

One of Luce Irigaray's main philosophic encounters has been with Friedrich Nietzsche. Irigaray's rewriting of Nietzsche, *Amante marine: De Friedrich Nietzsche*, has itself been the subject of much critical attention. Irigaray takes on, in "Speaking of Immemorial Waters" (the first of three parts), the Nietzsche of *Thus Spoke Zarathustra*; in the second part, "Veiled Lips", Irigaray considers Nietzsche's concept of *such geben als, se donner pour*, the self-giving of woman and truth; the third section, "When Gods Are Born", tackles the deities Apollo, Dionysus and Christ.

Luce Irigaray's treatment of Friedrich Nietzsche, however, is not straightforward, but multi-layered, ironic and lyrical. She writes not in a purely essay, lecture, novelistic or philosophical form. The problem of the 'feminine' and 'feminism' in Nietzsche's work, which Irigaray, Hélène Cixous and other feminists have analyzed, is a complex one. 'Perhaps I am the first psychologist of the eternally feminine', Nietzsche wonders in *Ecce Homo*.[12] For some feminist critics, though, Nietzsche's texts cannot be rescued from their sexist views on women and gender.[13] The Nietzschean project of the self-giving woman, the spiritually pregnant woman, forms a model for the (male) 'birther', an artist, who will become a 'birther', if he is lucky enough. Nietzsche saw in 'spiritual pregnancy' a way into the contemplative personality type, or the 'male mother'.[14] Irigaray does agree with Nietzsche on the subject of 'spiritual pregnancy' in "Ecce Mulier":

> Assurément la fécondité spirituelle existe. Elle a lieu parfois en deça ou au-déla de tout discours. [Certainly spiritual fecundity exists. It sometimes occurs before or beyond all discourse] (EM, 318-9)

JACQUES LACAN AND FRENCH FEMINISM

For French feminists such as Hélène Cixous, Jacques Lacan's (1901-81) philosophy of the Lacanian 'lack' is ridiculous. As she writes in "The Laugh of the Medusa": '[w]hat's a desire originating from a lack? A pretty meagre desire' (M, 262). Woman is man's dream, his desire, Cixous says, because she is absent: '[m]an's dream: I love her - absent, hence desirable, a dependent nonentity, hence adorable. Because she isn't there where she is' (NBW, 67). And Luce Irigaray and other feminists (Sarah Kofman, Elizabeth Grosz, Michèle Montrelay and Mary Ann Doane) have criticized the Freudian-Lacanian emphasis on the phallus as the 'transcendental signifier', as the measure of authentic sexual pleasure.[1] What woman lacks is lack itself, says Montrelay, an inability to create distance and representation.

From Plato to Sigmund Freud and Jacques Lacan the desire and lack has been central to Western sexual metaphysics: in this negative model, one is doomed to a desire for more and more consumption, which leads to dissatisfaction. Freudian-Lacanian desire can never be satisfied: dissatisfaction is built-in. Desire is never annihilated: for Georg Wilhelm Hegel, only another desire can satisfy desire and also perpetuate it. Desire thus desires more desire (this has a vivid expression in late capitalist consumerism, where it is always the *next* commodity that will truly satisfy and stop the hunger for more objects. But it never happens).

Far better to see desire, as Elizabeth Grosz does, as a positive force, one which (following Benedictus de Spinoza and Friedrich Nietzsche as opposed to Hegel and Freud), makes connections and alliances. Instead of regarding desire as a repetitive search for something to make up for a central, gaping loss, it is seen as a force of production and creative assemblage; not fantasmatic but real.[2] This view of desire (in the work of Nietzsche, Spinoza, Gilles Deleuze and Félix Guattari) is also that of Hélène Cixous and Luce Irigaray (Julia Kristeva seems to be less convinced, and more committed to a post-Lacanian reading of desire). Desire becomes not yearning but actualization, actions, creation: instead of a Lacanian lack, desire becomes primary. As Cixous says: 'my desires have invented new desires' (M, 246).

Hélène Cixous was critical of Jacques Lacan's view of women's sexuality; Lacan, Cixous said, thought women had nothing to say about their sexual pleasure, but that was because he couldn't hear what they were saying. Cixous says that women do have things to say about their *jouissance*, and they should speak up. Cixous has tried to do her own bit in expressing women's views (EHC, 158). 'Write! Writing is for you, you are for you' is Cixous' battle-cry in "The Laugh of the Medusa".

✤

The Lacanian Look emphasizes eroticism. Seeing is erotic, the eye becomes a kind of phallus, caressing the obscure object of desire, which it can never 'possess'. As the poet Rainer Maria Rilke wrote: '[g]azing is a wonderful thing.'[3] The act of looking eroticizes the object. Jack Zipes explains:

> For [Lacan], seeing is desire, and the eye functions as a kind of phallus. However, the eye cannot clearly see its object of desire, and in the case of

> male desire, the female object of desire is an illusion created by the male unconscious. Or, in other words, the male desire for woman expressed in the gaze is auto-erotic and involves the male's desire to have his own identity reconfirmed in a mirror image. (1986, 258)

The Look is an assertion of male power and sexuality. For the gaze is male, or masculine, and feminists have grappled with the notion of a female gaze.[4] 'Male desire is presented as a response to female beauty', writes Andrea Dworkin (*Intercourse*, 114). Lacanian psychoanalysis is a hell of misrepresentations and misreadings, mirrors and imaginary spaces. The subject in the Lacanian system is constantly trying to make good mistakes made in its early psycho-sexual growth. In the dreaded mirror phase, the image becomes a mirage, and a distance is set up between the image and the body, an absence which Lacan termed the *objet a*. In the confusions of the three realms, the symbolic, real and imaginary, the subject cannot realize what it most wants to realize. The objects of desire remain forever elusive.

There is something inexplicably depressing about Jacques Lacan's version of psycho-sexual events. Lovers, in the Lacanian system, desire what they cannot have. The problem of the lack, the *objet a* and *la chose*, can never be resolved. Lacanian philosophy posits, among other things (here we go again): an eternal search for what can never be found.[5] The Freudian-Lacanian system demands a continuous series of substitutions for objects to fill the primordial lack. It is a system of replacing an imaginary and immobile plenitude that will always fail. The primal realm remains always lost or forbidden. The Paradise of early childhood recedes ever further into the distance of the past.

Meanwhile, in the Jungian system, Beatrice, Laura, Cleopatra, Isolde, Eurydice, Ariadne and all those women of myth, poetry and legend, are incarnations of the *anima*, which is, as Carl Jung explains, something all males possess: '[e]very man carries with him the eternal image of woman, not the image of this or that particular woman, but a definitive feminine image.'[6] The *anima* is 'a personification of the unconscious in a man, which appears as a woman or a goddess in dreams, visions and creative fantasies', comment Emma Jung and Marie-Louise von Franz.[7] Male painters throughout history have depicted their version of the *anima*, it seems. Each (male) painter has a version of the 'inner feminine figure' as Jung called her (1967, 210-1). For painters, this idealized *anima* figure seems to be another manifestation of that obscure object of desire, the eroticized woman, a mirror for male lust. The equation is: the more sublime and voluptuous the woman is painted, the more sublime and voluptuous is the artist's desire. The artist's model, then, can be seen as a Jungian *anima*, heavily eroticized, a Lacanian phallic mirror. In *The Newly Born Woman*, Hélène Cixous speaks of Heinrich von Kleist's relation to the feminine, which describes her view of the poet's use of the unconscious and dreams, which is the realm of women (recalling Jung's concept of the *anima*). Kleist

> pursues her a long long time, yet she is in him, always has been in him, like a wound, like his own wound, like the wound he is and that creates him. In him she is the delightful, cruel irruption of the other, of the feminine one he carries, he makes, of whom he is a part, whose place he is, woman – or poetry – woman as the source of creation, part of him. His femininity is that part of him, the man, the lover, the poet, that always *escapes* him. Painfully, deliciously. (NBW, 115)

Further; in Lacanian psychology, desire, which is the foundation of the system, is enmeshed with speaking, with creativity and art. The œdipal crisis and the repression of the desire for the mother occurs with the entry into the Symbolic Order, and the entry into language. As Toril Moi crystallizes Jacques Lacan's thought so concisely in *French Feminist Thought*: '[t]o speak as a subject is therefore the same as to represent the existence of repressed desire' (1988, 99-100). The links between seeing and erotic pleasure, between the eye and the phallus, are found in much of Western 'high culture': not only in the history of painting, but also in the great works of poets such as Dante Alighieri, Francesco Petrarch, William Shakespeare and the troubadours. In the 'classic' text of pornography, Georges Bataille's *The Story of the Eye*, there are eyes placed in mouths, vulvas and anuses. Bataille takes the Sadeian ethic of the pornographic Look to its logical, literal extreme.[8]

Men gaze at women and manipulate them into erotic poses. Larysa Mykyta writes in 1983:

> The sexual triumph of the male passes through the eye, through the contemplation of the woman. Seeing the women ensures the satisfaction of wanting to be seen, of having one's desire recognized, and thus comes back to the original aim of the scopic drive. Woman is repressed as subject and desired as object in order to efface the gaze of the Other, the gaze that would destroy the illusion of reciprocity and oneness that the process of seeing usually supports. The female object does not look, does not have it own point of view; rather it is erected as an image of the phallus sustaining male desire.[9]

The pleasure of the text, whether the text is a painting, film, magazine, photograph, piece of theatre, and so on, comes, according to Roland Barthes, when the Look of the spectator is aligned with that of the author.[10] What feminist criticism has done is to question the masculine 'pleasure of the text', arguing for a feminist reading of the traditional masculine or patriarchal view of texts.

For some feminists, however, there can be no true 'feminist gaze', because the Look is always masculine, ultimately. If the spectator is a 'gendered object', suggests Annette Kuhn in *Women's Pictures: Feminism and the Cinema*, then 'masculine subjectivity '[is] the only subjectivity available' (1982, 63). The politics of representation, which are central to the consumption of culture and art, are weighted firmly in favour of men and patriarchy. As John Berger writes: 'men act and women appear'. And as Catherine King notes:

> most images in masculine visual ideology are created to empower men as spectators – that is, to see themselves as endlessly important with things laid out for their desire.[11]

Post-Lacanian feminists such as Luce Irigaray argue that subjectivity can only be attributed to women with difficulty. Irigaray claims that 'any theory of the subject has always been appropriated by the 'masculine'' (*Speculum*, 133). 'Woman' is tied to a 'non-subjective subjectum' (*Speculum*, 265). Irigaray stresses the sexed being, the sexualized subject and speaking position. No form of knowledge or philosophy can be authentic or 'universal' if it ignores the female position.

Luce Irigaray concentrates on the act of enunciation, the act of producing discourse. Irigaray stresses the interiority of the speaking subject, the traces of subjectivity found in acts of communication. The continual denial of a sexualized discourse threatens the possibility of an emergent non-patriarchal society. Irigaray has investigated the use by men and women of everyday language, concluding that men and women privilege different patterns of speech, with men encouraging their 'self-affection', or relations to/ with the self and the self projecting in others, while women use language to make connections and relationships with both sexes. Irigaray's deconstruction of the languages of science, philosophy and politics has demonstrated the repression of the feminine – Dale Spender and other feminists have come to similar conclusions. For Irigaray, this repression is not built into language, but reflects the (patriarchal) social order. In order to change one the other must also be changed.

Luce Irigaray says that if the vagina is regarded as a 'hole', it is a 'negative' space that cannot be represented in the dominant discourse: thus to have a vagina is to be deprived of a voice, to be decentred or culturally subordinated, and so Irigaray replaces Jacques Lacan's mirror with a vaginal speculum.[13] The phallic privileging of the masculine 'I' (penis, phallus, power, identity, and soul), means that female sexuality is rendered 'invisible', just as the vagina is a negative space or void. The phallus is the divine, beloved mirror, emblem of masculine narcissism. But the vulva, being a 'black hole', can reflect back nothing. There is no self there. Male speculations and narcissistic gazes create a male subject: the mistakes arise when this male subject is equated with the whole world. The universality of philosophy and psychoanalysis thus becomes founded on a one-sided (male) view of the world. Male sexuality and narcissism mistakenly become the basis for the universal model of sexuality in psychoanalysis. Female sexuality becomes the negative image of male sexuality, if female subjectivity is considered at all. Women are supposed to have 'penis envy', a hankering for the transcendent signifier which will enable them to attain a positive, creative identity. Freudian 'penis envy' has been rejected by most feminists.

One can see how Luce Irigaray would have upset Jacques Lacan, who founded his theory of sexuality, like Sigmund Freud, on the primary of the phallus. In the Freudian-Lacanian phallic system, all is unity, identity, singularity (all the way back to that initial 'singularity', the Big Bang). Ambiguity, multiplicity and excess are excluded from this view: Irigaray's project of rewriting Freud and Lacan disrupts the isomorphic unity and replaces it with a series of dense, poetic, parodic discourses, in which female repression is unleashed and the female unconscious is allowed to explode into academic patriarchy.

Luce Irigaray's specular project disrupts the insistence in phallic, patriarchal sexuality on one organ (penis), one orgasm or pleasure (male), one identity (male), and one model of representation (masculine). Irigaray's notion of feminine writing disrupts the unitary dimensions of the phallocratic system ('there would be no longer either subject or object', Irigaray wrote of the new 'female syntax' in *This Sex Which Is Not One*, and "oneness' would no longer be privileged' [134]).

For Madeleine Gagnon, the phallus is a symbol of political as well as psychological oppression for feminists: the phallus 'represents repressive capitalist ownership, the exploiting bourgeois, the higher knowledge that must be gotten over'. It means regimentation, representation, and perfection (M, 180). But there is also the fact that using genitals as models for exploring psychology, politics and society is full of problems - not the least being that focussing on the vulva as a 'hole' or void, which it plainly isn't, and the penis as the 'transcendent signifier', which it plainly isn't, is very silly. And of limited use, in the end.

3

FRENCH FEMINISM, SEXUALITY, AND SEXUAL DIFFERENCE

SEXUAL DIFFERENCE

When feminists discuss the body and sexuality, the results are just as controversial as their discussions of issues such as art vs. pornography, or the ways in which female power can be asserted in the social and political arena. Many feminists speak of the sexual superiority of women, or, if not 'superiority', then at least a sexuality that is more sophisticated, more dangerous, more exhilarating, more subtle, and more sensual - well, that amounts to 'superior'. For instance, Xavière Gauthier, a contemporary of Hélène Cixous, Luce Irigaray and Julia Kristeva, says that:

> ...witches [women] are bursting; their entire bodies are desire; their gestures are caresses; their smell, taste, hearing are all sensual. Their pleasure is so violent, so transgressive, so open, so fatal, that men have not yet recovered... Female eroticism is terrifying; it is an earthquake, a volcanic eruption, a tidal wave. It is disquieting and so is mystified. It is made a mystery.[1]

This transgressive, terrifying eroticism has not yet really been depicted in art or pornography for feminists. What one gets is men's version of it – male ideas of wild eroticism, with violence as a recurring ingredient. Hélène Cixous reckons that women have an 'infinite', 'cosmic' libido, an eroticism which is always in flux, and so minute and subtle, it goes far beyond male/ masculine sexuality.

> Almost everything is yet to be written by women about femininity: about their sexuality, that is, its infinite and mobile complexity, about their eroticization, sudden turn-ons of a certain miniscule-immense area of their bodies; not about destiny, but about the adventure of such and such a drive, about trips, crossings, trudges, abrupt and gradual awakenings, discoveries of a zone at one time timorous and soon to be forthright. A woman's body, with its thousand and one thresholds of ardor... (M, 256)

Women have an all-over, total body eroticism, say writers such as Anaïs Nin, Peter Redgrove and Luce Irigaray (and so do some men!). 'But *woman has sex organs just about everywhere*. She experiences pleasure almost everywhere', writes Luce Irigaray (yes, but so do many men!).[2] Feminists have spoken of the wildness of women's eroticism and their fantasies. What this stance does is to uphold the eternal philosophical dualism of the West, setting women always against men, and using men to gauge women's sexuality. Feminists such as Hélène Cixous have argued, rightly, that masculine 'binary logic', which constantly opposes terms such as 'masculine' and 'feminine', is very limiting. It is two-term logocentrism, which reduces everything to 'yes' or 'no' (*The Newly Born Woman*, 63f).

Some feminists have disagreed with Luce Irigaray's view of female sexuality, because she over-emphasizes eroticism, at the expense of other aspects: '[a]ll that 'is' woman comes to [Irigaray] in the last instances from her anatomical sex, which touches itself all the time. Poor woman' (M. Plaza, 32).

Love and sex in the traditional social system means for men a 'phallocentric narcissism', in which men must gain 'more masculinity: plus-value of virility, authority, power, money, or pleasure' (NBW, 44). The system favours men, but men are trapped in the process too, as well as women. However, it is women, Hélène Cixous claims in *Extreme Fidelity*, who have more chance of getting in contact with pleasure, due to sexual difference, due to the socio-cultural division of men and women. Also, Cixous says, women are more in touch with an experience of the 'inside', 'an experience of the capacity for other, an experience of non-negative change brought about by the other, of positive receptivity' (EF, 135).

Pornography, like art, pivots around *desire.* And desire, as Hélène Cixous notes, is something that never dies: '[d]esire never dies', she says (NBW). Cixous asks in *The Newly Born Woman*:

> How do I experience my sexual pleasure?... What is feminine *jouissance*, where is it sited, how is it inscribed in her body, in her unconscious? And then, how can it be written? (151)

The problem is that *jouissance* operates outside of culture or language: but, to use *jouissance*, to wield its power, some critics claim, one has to incorporate it somehow into language and expression. The radical otherness of *jouissance* becomes distorted and circumscribed if it continues to remain outside of language, or in the body (C. Duchen, 98). For Cixous, men are estranged from *jouissance* – or at least the feminine kind. 'I do not see how men talk about feminine *jouissance*. That is precisely what devours them' (EHC, 157).

Julia Kristeva writes in *About Chinese Women* that:

> no other civilization seems to have made the principle of sexual difference so crystal clear: between the two sexes a cleavage or abyss opens up... Monotheistic unity is sustained by a radical separation of the sexes: indeed, it is this very separation which is its prerequisite. (K, 141)

An extreme feminist position can be a little impractical, as Hélène Cixous pointed out, thinking back to the 1960s and 1970s:

> I wondered how these feminists could possibly hope to get through life because everything had been invented by men. It was like saying, 'we can't go by plane because a woman didn't invent it. (S. Sellers, 1988, 144)

One of the most fiercely contended areas of feminism, gay, lesbian, and queer theory, women's studies, and gender studies (whatever one wants to call it), is the issue of sexuality, and how it relates to gender, identity, art, pornography, representation, ideology, and politics. In the realm of feminism and gender/ gay/ lesbian/ queer sexuality studies, there is no single narrative thread to follow, but a bewilderingly intricate web of strands, layers, spaces and realms. The brief discussion that follows of sexual difference/ sexuality/ identity/ gender issues will not proceed in a satisfyingly logical and A to B to Z fashion, but in a circular, perhaps spiral, certainly a squiggly way. In gender/ gay/ lesbian/ queer/ sexuality/ women's studies, what one finds are the commentators, feminists and writers revolving and rehearsing and gassing about the same issues, time after time.

The trouble with comparing male and female sensuality is that women's sensuality is usually defined *in opposition to* men's sensuality, and in terms of heterosexuality. Hélène Cixous shows how limiting it is to speak in terms of 'woman' and 'man' (NBW, in M, 90f). Cixous' Derridan analysis reveals how duality upholds the patriarchal status quo. By stressing the sexual superiority of women, feminists acknowledge male sexuality as the only alternative, as the 'guide' by which to judge female sexuality. Sexual stereotypes are thus endorsed. Instead of men and women one may get reductions to the clitoris and penis. But lovemaking is more than genitals. People are more than that. Sex is more than the rubbing together of penis and clitoris. It may be better to speak of *difference,* as Monique Wittig and Bonnie Zimmerman suggest (in S. Munt, 3-6).

The sexual over-emphasis can be a problem. By reducing people to erotic creatures their potential can be limited. Sigmund Freud did this by sexualizing everything. In the Freudian view (which is also that of the Marquis de Sade, Charles Baudelaire, Georges Bataille, and others), the whole world is erotic – caves are vaginas, towers are phalloi. For the intellectuals, sex and death combine, and everything is reducible to sex and death ('birth, copulation and death', said T.S. Eliot, summarizing the cynical, oh so clever masculinist view). All this can be severely reductive, squashing the life out of life. sometimes evokes sexuality in a similar way to Bataille and Baudelaire.

Luce Irigaray in her famous description of women's sexuality says women have an all-over eroticism, a total body sensuality, where the whole of the skin is alive to touches. 'The whole of my body is sexuate. My sexuality isn't restricted to my sex and to the sexual act (in the narrow sense)', writes Irigaray (Je, 53). For Irigaray, a woman's sex is 'two lips which embrace continually', in which women are parthenogenic, and self-contained, not needing others to pleasure them, because 'they are pleasuring themselves – continually'.

For some feminists, Luce Irigaray's morphology of female creativity is empowering, 'a challenge to the traditional construction of feminine morphology where the bodies of women are seen as receptacles for masculine completeness.'[3] Other feminists see the emphasis on just one form of female sexuality as a distinctly reductive and inauthentic kind of feminism:

> If we define female subjectivity through universal biological/ libidinal givens [writes Ann Rosalind Jones], what happens to the project of changing the world in feminist directions? Further, is women's sexuality so monolithic that shared, typical femininity does justice to it? What about variations in class, in race, and in culture among women? about changes over time in *one* woman's sexuality? (with men, with women, by herself?) How can one libidinal voice – or the two vulval lips so startlingly presented by Irigaray – speak for all women?[4]

Hélène Cixous insists that she is not talking about anatomy or biology; it is history (personal and collective) and culture that determines how people respond in sexual relationships; it is

> the way the individual negotiates with these schema, with these data, adapts to them and reproduces them, or else gets round them, overcomes them, goes beyond them, gets through them. (EF, 135)

Chris Straayer writes:

> The Hollywood romance formula of love at first sight relies on a slippage between sexuality and love. Sexual desire pretends to be reason enough for love, and love pretends to be sexual pleasure. While sexual desire is visually available for viewer's vicarious experiences, sexual pleasure is blocked. By the time the plot reaches a symbolic climax, love has been substituted for sex, restricting sex to the realm of desire. So structured, love is unrequited sex.[5]

Some feminists (such as Anaïs Nin and Hélène Cixous) argue for multiple sexualities, for a plurality of sexualities, as against the standard, traditional notions of heterosexuality, homosexuality, lesbianism and bisexuality. Some feminists argue for the use of erotic feeling as a political weapon. Instead of denying eroticism, some feminists propound an ethics of glorifying sexuality. The body then becomes the centre, the subject, instead of being merely the object of male lust. Eroticism then becomes a source of power, as Audre Lorde explains:

> The erotic is a resource within each of us that lies in a deeply female and spiritual plane, firmly rooted in the power of our unexpressed or unrecognized feeling.[6]

In *The Book of Promethea*, Hélène Cixous speaks of wishing to enter another body, the 'you' of the book. To 'sink into her body, slow and breathless to go down inside her heaving breast'. Of wanting to go in under the skin, where there is no skin, no edge, no boundaries, into the naked you ('you are so nakedly naked, so glowing'), so that she is 'already hip-deep in your eyes, I am already breast-deep in your soul. You are so wide open.' The body of the beloved is all inside and outside, a 'dizzying land', the 'deep body' of honey, wine, blood, a meshing of lips and breasts (BP, 112-3). Cixous' writing is already deeply erotic: it does not need to mention genitals or fucking; it is already there. Like many writers, Cixous does write in a deliberately erotic mode at times, in *Breaths*:

> I do not swallow her like your saliva; I do not suckle her, I do not kiss her with the tenderness that swells the lips of my cunt when it embraces your penis; nothing of our approximations, of our penetrations, our capturings. Not our oracles. She does not dissolve. Host, cake, seed, sperm, poppy-seed cake, man's milk, my delights, she is not that. (C, 51)

In *La Jeune Née* Hélène Cixous plays with the word 'cunt': '[s]he must recognize and recuntize the male partner', she writes; 'All women have more or less experienced this cuntditionality of masculine desire. And all its secuntdary effects' (NBW, 80-81). Valerie Traub notes that kissing is 'widely construed as a synecdoche of the movements of the erotic body, indeed, the sine qua non of erotic desire'.[7] Prostitutes prefer to avoid kissing, it is suggested, because kissing 'imports emotion into a commercial transaction' (ib., 135). Kissing is not depicted often in pornography, a critic suggests, because it brings emotion in, and disrupts the fantasy of unbridled desire.[8]

Using the terms of Freudian psychoanalysis, Hélène Cixous says in an interview that the individual must move from the anal and oral psychosexual stages to the genital. The 'full, total, accomplished individual goes through all the stages and arrives at the genital stage that assembles everything'.

For Hélène Cixous, the anal stage is avaricious, retentive, hard, dominating; people at the oral stage 'have a censoring relationship to others'. But the

> ideal harmony, reached by few, would be genital, assembling everything and being capable of generosity, of spending. That is what I mean when I speak of *l'écriture féminine*, that is what I talk about. (EHC, 131)

Attaining it is rare, however. So is the feminine libidinal economy, the 'one that tolerates the movements of the other, is very rare: one that tolerates the comings and goings, the movements, the space' (EHC, 137). Women have more of a chance of attaining a real love than men, Cixous says, because society rejects the possibility for men:

> Society does not give you any time. You have just lived through an experience, and society tells you that if you believe that, you should get lost; there is no place for you.

However, women have a chance in the quest for real love because

> for culturally negative reasons they are not called upon, they are not obligated to participate in the big social *fête* – which is phallocentric – since they are often given places in the shadow, places of retreat (EHC, 134)

Hélène Cixous dislikes dualistic terms such as 'masculine' and 'feminine' – she wishes to do away with them (EHC, 129). In Cixous' view of sexual relations, a wholly masculine or wholly feminine kind of sexuality is too limiting; there must be no immovable sexual opposition either. Instead,

> there is exchange. As soon as you simply touch the other, you alter the other and you are altered by the other, an alteration that may be positive or negative. (EHC, 136)

Love often consists in letting oneself be changed, in order 'to feel the other of the other' (ibid.).

Women speak of their eroticism in fiction and fantasy as being multi-sensual, not simply a matter of the visual or haptic senses, but of every sense, and more, in a synæsthetic experience.

> In those early mornings it all tasted of sex after a few moments... The whole room seemed full of our commingled, complicated smells. And over and over again I'd come, sometimes still nearly asleep

wrote Sue Miller in *The Good Mother*,[9] while Summer Brenner remarked: 'our bodies made light in a soft room'.[10] Susan Griffin has written powerfully of lesbian eroticism in *Viyella*:

> ...my most profound longings and desires, for intimacy, to know, to touch and be inside the body and soul of another, becoming and separating from, devouring and being devoured, that wild, large, amazing, frightening territory of lovemaking belongs for me not with men, but with women.[11]

Nancy Friday has collected women's fantasies in a number of books: *My Secret Garden, Women On Top* and *Forbidden Flowers.* The fantasies involve lesbianism, group sex, sex with animals, sex with pop and movie stars, rape, anal sex, domination, S/M and all manner of erotic activities. Women's fantasies, like their fictions, are, some feminists believe, wilder, larger, more amazing and more frightening, to use Susan Griffin's words, than male fantasies and fictions.[12]

The books of erotic fiction and fantasy by women demonstrate something of the erotic ecstasy of women which, as Xavière Gauthier writes, 'is so violent, so transgressive, so open, so fatal, that men have not yet recovered.'[13]

Liz Kotz has pointed out: 'representing fantasmatic processes with complex relations to the real.' Kotz is discussing pornography and art, but her analysis applies to the media.[14] Fantasy is useful for writers aiming to explore 'female' experience, for in fantasy there may be the possibility that non-establishment material may come through. Fantasy may allow women to 'speak female desire as multiplicity, joyousness, pleasure, *jouissance*', as Roland Barthes put it.[15] While masculine culture exalts 'realism' and 'rationality', fantasy perhaps offers a platform for non-patriarchal material.

Luce Irigaray talks about the 'very openness' of women's bodies, 'of their flesh, of their genitals', so that boundaries become difficult to define (I, 112). Irigaray speaks of two kinds of erotic *jouissance* – the phallic kind of orgasm, which men are concerned with and brag about – and the *jouissance* in harmony with a female libidinal economy (I, 45). Irigaray's point is that there are forms of *jouissance* other than the phallocratic model. Incredible though women's sexual fantasies may be, they are always defined in terms of male fantasies, often in terms of difference. Julia Kristeva's form of *jouissance* is not Jacques Lacan's phallic or sexual *jouissance*, but a *jouissance* that is ecstasy. For erotic pleasure, Kristeva uses the term *plaisir* (DL, 160).

LESBIAN, GAY AND QUEER THEORY; MONIQUE WITTIG AND FRENCH FEMINISM

Lesbian, gay and queer cultural theory has continually addressed the problem of identity and gender. There are certain sexual and social 'positions' or 'categories' which are seen as 'outside' the (patriarchal) norms, which may have affinities with the female 'outsider' figures of Julia Kristeva and Luce Irigaray. The lesbian, for instance, is sometimes seen as an 'outsider', like the black woman, or the feminist. Gender and sexual identity categories are becoming increasingly blurred.

For example, there are

- 'physical' lesbians,
- 'natural' lesbians,
- 'cultural' or 'social' lesbians,
- 'male' lesbians (men who position themselves as lesbians).
- men with vaginas and women with penises;
- there are queer butches and aggressive femmes,
- there are F2Ms and lesbians who love men,
- queer queens and drag kings,
- daddy boys and dyke mummies,
- bull daggers,
- porno afro homos,
- transsexual Asians,
- butch bottoms,
- femme tops,
- women and lesbians who fuck men,
- women and lesbians who fuck *like* men,
- lesbians who dress up as men impersonating women,
- lesbians who dress up as straight men in order to pick up gay men,
- butches who dress in fem clothing to feel like a gay man dressing as a woman,
- femmes butched-out in male drag
- and butches femmed-out in drag.

Sexual and social identities are continually being blurred, redefined, performed, questioned. Terms such as 'straight' and 'gay', 'hetero' and 'homo'/ 'hommo', are no longer adequate for these multi-layered, post-modern sexual identities. We need multiple genders - millions of genders. Two or three just ain't enough! There are many sexualities - surely as many as there are people, and also more (some people have multiple sexualities).

In lesbian and queer theory there are debates about the penis and the phallus: should lesbian sex involve penetration, which merely mimes heterosexual intercourse and perhaps upholds patriarchal norms? Is the lesbian use of the dildo 'subversive' or a parody? Does lesbian S/M mock or emulate straight sex? Is the lesbian butch/ femme social category simplistic and stereotypical? Is lesbian sexuality truly 'outside' patriarchal/ masculinist sexuality? These are the concerns also of Hélène Cixous, Luce Irigaray and Julia Kristeva - the project of an erotic otherness, of an outside space or wild zone for women, a sexuality undefined and unfettered by masculinist discourse. Cixous especially (in "The Laugh of the Medusa"), has argued for a transgressive, radical, political and passionate form of female sexuality, which will go beyond male sexuality. The project is for a female sexuality that will not be a duplicate of masculinist sexuality, that will go beyond male narcissism, doubling and self-recognition.

In the 'lesbian dildo debates', questions are asked such as does the dildo *always* refer to the penis? Does a dildo have to be lifelike? Why? Is a lifelike dildo more 'authentic', more valuable, than an obviously 'artificial-looking' one? Is using the dildo 'patriarchal'? Or 'masculine'? Is someone using a dildo or a strap-on 'masculine'? Are they purveying patriarchal notions of penetration and domination?[1]

The lesbian sexologist Susie Bright (Susie Sexpert) downplays the relation between the dildo and the penis. She says that a dildo is simply an object that takes up space in the vagina or anus, that it can be a 'succulent squash, or a tender mould of silicon'. In male gay sex and pornography, a dildo definitely does refer to the penis. There are even dildos which are modelled on particular penises, such as porn star Jeff Stryker. Thus one could be fucked by a copy of one's favourite star's penis. This recalls the Chicago groupies, the Plastercasters, who took plaster casts of rock star's penises. Flesh-coloured penises are in fact cream coloured. But the biggest seller among dildos is apparently large black dildos. Some of these, such as the 'Big Black Dick', are 24 inches long. Here sexual practices merge into issues of race. One can pretend being fucked by a black man while using the 'Big Black Dick'. 'As in the case of Freud's fetishist and his "woman," the big black dildo allows whites to carry on a relation with blacks that is, in reality, no relation at all' (H. Findlay, op. cit., 335).

Some critics relate the dildo to the Freudian missing phallus of the mother. The dildo may be the Freudian fetish: Freud suggested that the fetish 'is a substitute for the woman's (the mother's) penis that the little boy once believed in'.[2] XX Putting on a harness and fastening a dildo may be a way of rehearsing 'in a literal manner, the traumatic primal experience of Freud's little fetishist: now she has it, now she doesn't' (H. Findlay, op.cit., 334).

Monique Wittig (1935-2003) is another powerful French feminist whose works, like those of Hélène Cixous, Luce Irigaray and Julia Kristeva, have been influential and controversial in the field of feminist cultural debate. Wittig is sometimes grouped with Irigaray and Cixous and the project of *écriture féminine*, but Wittig's view of 'lesbian writing' is not about exalting female difference, for in 'lesbian writing' sex is eliminated as a category. Wittig's works (*Les Guerillères, L'Opoponax, The Lesbian Body,* "The Straight Mind", "One Is Not Born a Woman", and *Virigile, non, Brouillon pour un dictionaire des amantes*), seem to offer a radical view of lesbians. Wittig positions lesbians somewhat as Kristeva and Cixous position women: as societal outsiders. In "The Straight Mind", Wittig sees lesbians as becoming nomads and runaways, as well as becoming more establishment. For Wittig, lesbians are outsiders in the hetero-patriarchal system: Wittig's oft-quoted statement runs thus:

> Lesbian is the only concept I know of which is beyond the categories of sex (woman and man), because the designated subject (lesbian) is *not* a woman, either economically, or politically, or ideologically. (1980, 53)

In *Le corps lesbien,* Monique Wittig transformed the (male/ masculinist) 'I' of Western love poetry into the split 'J/e', the aim being to 'lesbianize the symbols' (1985, 11), so that Orphea saves her Euridice, and Christ becomes 'Christa the much-crucified'. For some feminists, Wittig has created in 'J/e' 'the most powerful lesbian in literature' (Elaine Marks);[3] Wittig's lesbian writings have created a new 'lesbian narrative space',[4] with an 'epistemological shift' away from phallocentrism.[5] xx Wittig's lesbian writing has nullified the masculinist social position (D. Crowder, 127).

For other feminists, Monique Wittig's project is simply too utopian and impractical: it makes the leap from imagination to representation without considering the practical difficulties of the proto-separatist lesbian utopia. Critics such as Judith Butler (in her book *Gender Trouble*) have seen that Wittig assumes a nostalgic once-upon-a-time social unity, which did not exist, and has never existed. Rather than rewriting or radically challenging notions of gender and sexuality, Wittig's texts affirm heterosexual and homosexual norms (1990, 115, 121). Wittig's view of lesbian sexuality and art is problematic: its relations to heteropatriarchy in particular are ambiguous. Wittig's texts, though, despite the confusions, offer an exuberant and thought-provoking revision of the heterosexual establishment.

Monique Wittig's lesbian philosophy is radical, in that she claims that lesbians are outside of heterosexual culture, and therefore the term 'woman' does not apply to them. In *Questions Féministes* in 1980, Wittig published an article ("The Straight Mind") which claimed that 'lesbians are not women' (1992, 32).

This form of (theoretical) lesbian separatism provides both a powerful position from which to speak, and an undermining of 'female' or 'women's' power. Being outside the group of (heterosexual) women could mean that it is difficult to change the heteropatriarchal system. For some feminists, one must work *within* the system in order to change it. Being a radical non-'woman' lesbian in Monique Wittig's view may render revolutionary change difficult. Making heterosexuality and men the 'enemy' as a whole, either socially or theoretically, renders some modes of change difficult, or even impossible. Radical lesbian separatism may be a position of power, but it is fraught with theoretical (and social, political and ideological) difficulties. Wittig does recognize the social angle of oppression ('[i]t is oppression that creates sex and not the contrary', she says [1992, 2]).

Some commentators have over-emphasized the sexual aspect of Monique Wittig's conception of heterosexuality. For example, Judith Butler in *Gender Trouble* has viewed Wittig's system of the binary sexual divide as 'serving the reproductive aims of a compulsory heterosexuality' (1990, 19). For Wittig, however, there is more to heterosexual oppression than sexual desire. There are also the social institutions of marriage and labour. Wittig writes (in 1982):

> The category of sex is the product of a heterosexual society in which men appropriate for themselves the reproduction and production of women and also their physical persons by means of...the marriage contract. (1992, 6)

Monique Wittig challenges conventional forms of the 'feminine' and language by

> not only reveal[ing] the violence done to women (entering language) but also turns the violence back on to language - the body of the text, of the word - and the body in the text. (J. Still, 1993, 24)

Simone de Beauvoir remarked of liberation for women: 'the first thing is work. Then refuse marriage if possible' (M, 147). In Luce Irigaray's view, women, in the psychoanalytic (Freudian/ Lacanian) system, are objects or commodities that are exchanged between men. Freudian œdipalization becomes in fact an economy of female trade between men. The significance of desire in Irigaray's reading of psychoanalytic sexual economy is not as a lack or focussed on particular objects (women), but a circuit of flows and paths, detours and dynamics. In this narcissistic, phallocentric monopoly, women are not the endpoint but the means or carriers of male desire. As it's between men, this sexual economy is homosexual, governed by and for men. The lesbian is thus a double negative in this social and metaphysical system: as a woman, she is silenced and negated; as a lesbian she disappears completely from the masculinist system of exchange. The lesbian subverts the economy of trade which is founded on the phallus.

WOMEN AS WITCHES, OUTSIDERS, POETS

In the Neoplatonic, Aristotlean, Renaissance view of the fine art establishment, there is good art and bad art, there is the art of 'taste', 'decency', 'refinement', 'purity' and 'civilization', and there is the vulgar, the uncouth, the disrespectful, the unornamental, the unlearned. In mediæval culture, there is Sacred and Profane Love, drawn from Plato's *Symposium*, and the figures of Venus Vulgaris (Earthly Venus) and Venus Coelestis. The Heavenly Venus is the one to aspire to, even though the Earthly Venus may be much more exciting. These dichotomies are found throughout art. There is the chaste, passive, motherly Virgin Mary and the sexual, active, lascivious Mary Magdalene.[1] There is good and evil. There is Heaven and Hell.

There is male and female.

Throughout the history of Western culture one comes across the same dualities, in one form or another. The female is clearly on the 'left' side, on the wrong side of the 'right' way. Women are the 'second sex', 'second class citizens': Sherry Ortner points out that there is an opposition between culture and nature, and women are lower down in the male-made hierarchy:

> my thesis is that woman is being identified with – or, if you will, seems to be a symbol of – something that every culture devalues, something that every culture defines as being of a lower order of existence than itself.[2]

Women are imprisoned, as Hélène Cixous notes, in masculine binary logic, which is the 'classical vision of sexual opposition between men and women', as Verena Conley writes in her book on Cixous (1984, 129). For Luce Irigaray, this duality is called 'the recto-verso structure that shores up common sense' (I, 127).

Feminists speak of experiences beyond male control: pregnancy, childbirth, female orgasm and *jouissance*. The sexual difference that should be celebrated by women, Hélène Cixous says, can derive from real or imagined experiences. For Cixous, *la jouissance féminine* (female sexual pleasure) is decentralized, vast, overflowing, like water. 'The body lets desires pass through and this desire creates images, fantasies and figures', writes Sarah Cornell (in H. Wilcox, 39). Julia Kristeva remarked in *About Chinese Women*:

> If a woman cannot be part of the temporal symbolic order except by identifying with the father, it is clear that as soon as she shows any sign of that which, in herself, escapes such identification and acts differently, resembling the dream of the maternal body, she evolves into this 'truth' in question. It is thus that female specificity defines itself in patrilinear society: woman is a specialist in the unconscious, a witch, a bacchanalian, taking her jouissance in an anti-Apollonian, Dionysian orgy. (K, 154)

Like the poet, woman is a shaman, a witch, a magician, moving beyond the symbolic/ œdipal/ patriarchal order; 'the female is the initiatrix', wrote Alex Comfort (1979). This is a continuing theme in the writings of Julia Kristeva. In "The True-Real" ("Le vréel"), she asserted:

> We know...how logic and ontology have inscribed the question of *truth*

> within *judgement* (or sentence structure) and *being,* dismissing as *madness, mysticism or poetry* any attempt to articulate that impossible element which henceforth can only be designated by the Lacanian category of the *real*. After the flowering of mysticism, classical rationality, first by embracing Folly with Erasmus, and then by excluding it with Descartes, attempted to enunciate the real as truth by setting limits on Madness; modernity, on the other hand, opens up this enclosure in a search for other forms capable of transforming or rehabilitating the statues of *truth*. (K, 217)

'We're stormy,' says Hélène Cixous (E. Marks, 245), and women are. For some feminists, it is not that women are not actually 'wilder and stranger' than men, in themselves, rather, women's *cultural space* is wilder and stranger. Feminists such as Elaine Showalter and Jeanne Roberts, taking their cue from Edwin Ardener,[3] propose that there is a female 'wild zone', as there is a male 'wild zone'. One knows about men's version of wild zone eroticism, what Cixous calls 'glorious phallic monosexuality' (M, 254): it's the stuff of legend, of hunting, of violence, brotherhoods, initiations, and so on. Female 'otherness' is beyond patriarchal space, beyond patriarchal representations.[4] Showalter in "Feminist Criticism in the Wilderness" suggests that, in terms of space, the female 'wild zone' 'is literally no-man's land, a place forbidden to men', while as (an) experience, it refers to aspects of women's life unavailable to or outside of male experience; metaphysically, it may be a space quite outside of masculine consciousness (ib., 262).

The female 'wild zone' is that moon-place/ womb-space of hysteria, menstrual madness, blood mysteries, women's adventures. The 'wild zone' is a cultural more than a biological space; that is, things experienced there are beyond established male culture, and a new language has to be invented to describe experiences in the female 'wild zone'. 'All desire is connected to madness', Luce Irigaray asserted in *Sexes et parentés* (I, 35).

Hélène Cixous wrote in "The Laugh of the Medusa" of women as outsiders or witches, living in the unconscious or the wilderness, who must return

> from afar, from always, from "without", from the heath where witches are kept alive; from below, from "beyond" culture... (M, 247)

Catherine Clément spoke of the sorceress or hysteric as ambiguous, anti-establishment yet conservative; who disrupts the establishment, the Church, who heals, performs abortions, uses magic, and who ends up being destroyed (NBW, 5). The witch 'serves to connect all the ends of a culture that is hard to endure', especially in a Christian society (ib., 8). 'The hysterics are my sisters', asserted Hélène Cixous (ib., 99). An outcast or sorceress, 'woman' may also exist within the traditional economies and languages. In Cixous' terms, 'woman' must be the darer, the one who 'goes and passes into infinity', the traveller who 'alone wishes to know from within', even though she is eternally the outcast (M, 260).

When she writes, Hélène Cixous says, she is a multiplicity of selves. 'I am haunted by others. I am all the others' (EHC, 175). Writing means being in a state of change, of travel. Though there is some self left, writing means being in 'a state of tension or of travel', so that the writer is 'in a plurality of worlds' (ibid.). Cixous was not always denigrating men; there were men, she said, that were capable of 'becoming woman'; for Cixous, these feminized men were the poets:

> There have been poets who let something different from tradition get through at any price – men able to love love; therefore, to love others, to want them; men able to think the woman who would resist destruction and constitute herself as a superb, equal, "impossible" subject. (NBW, 98).

Jacques Lacan called his notion of body image 'imaginary anatomy', which Elizabeth Grosz has defined in *Volatile Bodies* thus:

> The imaginary anatomy is an internalized image or map of the meaning that the body has for the subject, for others in its social world, and for the symbolic order in its generality (that is, for a culture as a whole). This, Lacan claims, helps to explain the peculiar, nonorganic connections formed in hysteria and in such phenomena as the phantom limb. It is also helps to explain why there are distinct waves of particular

> forms of hysteria (some even call them fashions), i.e., why hysteria commonly exhibited forms of breathing difficulty (e.g., fainting, tussis nervosa, breathlessness, etc) in the nineteenth century which, by comparison today, have relatively disappeared (perhaps with the exception of asthma and various "allergic" reactions) and yet why, taking their place as the most "popular" forms of hysteria today, are eating disorders, anorexia nervosa and bulimia in particular. (39-40)

Julia Kristeva and Luce Irigaray, among other French feminists, have spoken of something in women or the feminine that is 'unrepresentable', beyond art, beyond male culture. 'Woman' is always negative, always outside the symbolic realm; 'woman' 'isn't this (can't be defined), it isn't yet that (isn't yet here)', Claire Duchen noted in *Feminism in France From May '68 to Mitterand* (85).

This notion of 'woman' as 'outsider' is aligned to Julia Kristeva's notion of the *sujet-en-procès* and the 'negativity' of the text, which Kristeva developed in early works such as *Séméiotikè, La Révolution du langage poetique* and *Polylogue*. In *About Chinese Women*, Kristeva writes of the woman as a witch, someone outside of patriarchal discourse, or at least, thrown to the edge, the border between the known and the otherness:

> A *jouissance* which breaks the symbolic chain, the taboo, the mastery. A *marginal discourse*, with regard to the science, religion and philosophy of the *polis* (witch, child, under-developed, not even a poet, at best his accomplice). (K, 154)

Ann Rosalind Jones describes Julia Kristeva's notion of the 'outsider' culture of women, of women as 'witches':

> Women, for Kristeva... speak and write as "hysterics," as outsiders to male-dominated discourse, for two reasons: 'the pre-dominance in them of drives related to anality and childbirth, and their marginal position vis-à-vis masculine culture. Their semiotic style is likely to involve repetitive, spasmodic separations from the dominating discourse. which, more often, they are forced to imitate.[5]

For Alice Jardine, Julia Kristeva's notion of the Other or alterity always ends up with the other sex. The first Other may be the mother, but Kristeva, Jardine maintains, 'has repeatedly pointed out that the Other is always in fact the "other sex"', and in "Opaque Texts" Jardine quotes Kristeva in *Revolution in Poetic Language*: '[t]he difference between 'I' and 'you' turns out to be coextensive with the sexual difference' (1984, 326). Kristeva's female voice, though, Jardine asserts, is 'strangely subversive'.[6] Mme Cixous says that difference is not a product, not something tangible, that can be quantified and categorized; rather, difference passes through people, it 'crosses through us, like a goddess. We cannot capture it. It makes us teeter with emotion' ("Preface," C, xviii).

Julia Kristeva's writings may be the most coherent and incisive account of psychocultural 'otherness'. Victor Burgin, describing Kristeva's philosophy, says that she positions

> the woman in society... in the patriarchal, as perpetually at the boundary, the borderline, the edge, the 'outer limit' – the place where order shades into chaos, light into darkness. The peripheral and ambivalent position allocated to woman, says Kristeva, had led to that familiar division of the field of representation in which women are viewed as either saintly or demonic – according to whether they are seen as bringing the darkness, or as keeping it out[7]

Saintly woman (the Virgin Mary is a typical example) keeps the amazing energy of female otherness out of men's lives; the demonic woman (Mary Magdalene, the *femme fatale*, vampire, 'devil woman') is the one who brings the wildness with her. Patriarchy of course prefers bland, mute, passive doorstops in women, people who will stop the darkness from coming in, who will sit there and say nothing and get on with society's housework.

André Breton said that 'existence is elsewhere'. French feminists say that 'woman' is elsewhere. 'She is indefinitely other in herself,' comments Luce Irigaray, maintaining that women

> are already elsewhere than in the discursive machinery where you

> claim to take them by surprise. They have turned back within themselves, which does not mean the same thing as 'within yourself'. They do not experience the same interiority that you do and which perhaps you mistakenly presume they share. (*This Sex Which Is Not One*, 68-69)

Here, perhaps, is female 'otherness', some of the wildness and strangeness and ecstasy of female eroticism may be experienced and depicted. Luce Irigaray also spoke in spatial terms of idealist feminism:

> We need both space and time. And perhaps we are living in an age when *time must re-deploy space*. Could this be the dawning of a new world? Immanence and transcendence are being recast, notably by that *threshold* which has never been examined in itself: the female sex. It is a threshold unto *mucosity*. Beyond the classic opposites of love and hate, liquid and ice lies this perpetually *half-open* threshold, consisting of *lips* that are strangers to dichotomy. Pressed against one another, but without any possibility of suture, at least of a real kind, they do not absorb the world either into themselves or through themselves, provided they are not abused or reduced to a mere consummating or consuming structure. Instead their shape welcomes without assimilating or reducing or devouring. A sort of door unto voluptuousness, then? Not that, either: their useful function is to designate a *place*: the very place of uses, at least on a habitual plane. Strictly speaking, they serve neither conception nor *jouissance*. Is this, then, the mystery of female identity, of its self-contemplation, of that strange word of silence; both the threshold and reception of exchange, the sealed-up secret of wisdom, belief and faith in every truth?[8]

Many feminists suggest that women's eroticism cannot be represented, much as women themselves cannot be represented. Julia Kristeva writes: '[i]n "woman" I see something that cannot be represented, something that is not said, something above and beyond nomenclatures and ideologies.'[9] Other feminists echo this idea, that women cannot be fully represented in the traditional media of patriarchy. As Hélène Cixous writes:

> It is at the level of sexual pleasure in my opinion that the difference makes itself most clearly apparent in as far as woman's libidinal economy is neither identifiable by a man nor referrable to the masculine economy. ("Sorties", M, 95)

The unrepresentable in art and pornography, according to some feminists, is women's eroticism, their *jouissance*, that 'explosive, blossoming, sane and inexhaustible *jouissance* of the woman', as Julia Kristeva describes it in *About Chinese Women* (63). Richard Dyer, in "Male Gay Porn", reckons that gay pornography is not much different from straight porn because the desire to ejaculate is primary, rather than being fucked.[10] The typical sequence of events in both straight male and gay male pornography is foreplay then sucking then fucking, with a climax consisting of ejaculation outside the body.[11]

What one gets in most Western art, from Greek and Roman sculpture through the glories of the Renaissance to the latest pornography, are male representations of female eroticism. Feminists say that there are no real depictions of female *jouissance* in art or literature. 'In my opinion,' remarked Marguerite Duras, 'women have never expressed themselves.'[12] What she means, perhaps, is that women have expressed themselves thus far in the terms and means defined by men. There is no 'feminine' or 'women's' writing, according to some feminists. For Duras, 'the future belongs to women. Men have been completely dethroned' (M, 238).

On gay and heterosexual pornography, Thomas Waugh writes, *pace* Andrea Dworkin's view that all images of sex involve victimization (of women):

> Specific sexual practices as depicted in a given image do not necessarily coincide with relations of exploitation or domination, nor with any other power relation. A man or woman portrayed as getting fucked cannot automatically be seen as victim. (T. Waugh, op. cit., 313)

Real sex, the French feminists argue, has not yet been represented. Women haven't done it because they work within the same patriarchal structures, codes and constraints as men. Men, generally, haven't got a hope of depicting authentic female eroticism, although the authors of millions of pornographic products would claim they know everything about female eroticism. On the other hand, in the mechanisms of cultural and postmodern theory, anyone, male or female, should be able to create a truly 'feminine' text. It shouldn't matter who the author is. If the French feminists are right, then nearly all of the art produced anywhere is oriented to the male and the masculine, *even* when it is created by *women*. Many women artists would dispute this. The notion of an 'authentic' 'women's'/ 'feminine' art continues to be hotly debated.[13]

Écriture féminine is a subversive position and activity, which deconstructs patriarchal (phallogocentric) language (S. Hekman, 42). The 'sophisticated theoretical dilemma' of Hélène Cixous' project was whether a 'female' or 'feminine' voice could be envisaged without 'acquiring its own kind of phallocentricity' (J. Duran, 174). If the woman's voice became phallocentric it was as if she had picked up the phallus itself.[14] The fluid, plural and diffuse sense of 'feminine writing' subverts masculine culture (C. Burke, 1981, 289; J. Sayers, 1982, 132; C. Faure, 1981, 85).

Luce Irigaray privileges a poetry of women's laughter in the face of phallocracy; both Irigaray and Hélène Cixous advocate intimate, personal, precious languages of imaginary spaces that exist outside of phallocracy (L. Kipnis, 207). According to the French feminists, 'women's' or 'feminine' or 'female' art is created in the gaps and silences of a text, but not in the intentional space of the artwork. Mary Jacobus explains:

> The French insistence on *écriture féminine* – on woman as a writing-effect instead of an origin – asserts not the sexuality of the text but the textuality of sex. Gender difference, produced, not innate, becomes a matter of the structuring of a genderless libido in and through patriarchal discourse. Language itself would at once repress multiplicity and heterogeneity – true difference – by the tyranny of hierarchical oppositions (man/ woman) and simultaneously work to overthrow that tyranny by interrogating the limits of meaning. The 'feminine', in this scheme, is to be located in the gaps, the absences, the unsayable or unrepresentable of discourse and representation. (1982, 14, 1)

For some feminists, philosophies based on the body are problematic, because to look for some essential nature of 'woman', some essence based in biology, is dubious.[15] Indeed, Toril Moi says that 'to define 'woman' is necessarily to essentialize her' (1988, 139). Jacques Derrida had written in *Spurs* that

> There is no such thing as the essence of woman because woman averts, she is averted of herself. Out of the depths, endless and unfathomable, she engulfs and distorts all vestige of essentiality, of identity, of property. (51)

For some critics, Hélène Cixous' notion of 'woman' is *only* valorized in writing, and nowhere else (S. Wiseman, in H. Wilcox, 109). What is 'woman', anyway? A 'writing-effect', for the feminist Alice Jardine, an element in culture or a text. For Julia Kristeva, 'woman' does not 'exist', because there is no 'essence', no 'essential' woman (S. Hekman, 148). For Kristeva, not only 'woman' and the subject is 'in process' (*sujet-en-procès*), but the body and sexuality as well. French feminism produces a feminist 'space' rather than a 'sex'; the position is a cultural one, not, as in Anglo-American feminism, a discourse based on the biological woman. It's important, as Monique Wittig notes, to make a distinction between the various interpretations 'woman' and 'women':

> Our first task... is thoroughly to dissociate "woman" (the class within which we fight) and "woman," the myth. For "woman" does not exist for us; it is only an imaginary formation, while "women" is the duct of a social relationship.[16]

Elaine Showalter writes of the biologic and genderized views of feminism in "Feminist Criticism in the Wilderness":

> Organic or biological criticism is the most extreme statement of gender difference, of a text indelibly marked by the body: anatomy is textuality... Simply to invoke anatomy risks a return to the crude essentialism, the phallic and ovarian theories of art, that oppressed women in the past.[17]

Biology, though, is crucial; the body is crucial.[18] Hélène Cixous states: '[i]n censuring the body, one censures at the same time breathing and speech' (NBW, 179). And French feminist Madeleine Gagnon writes that '[a]ll we have to do is let the body flow, from the inside' (in M, 180). But feminists such as Elaine Showalter are wary of biologist or essentialist philosophies, especially those of French feminism (see also J. Sayers, 1986, 42; T. Moi, 1985, 110; H. Wenzel, 1981, 284; M. Plaza, 1978).

As Simone de Beauvoir put it, women are not born, they are made, meaning socially, culturally, politically, ideologically, psychologically, etc. For de Beauvoir, 'nature plays an infinitesimal role in the development of a human being': instead, it was socialization that made all of the difference; it was everything that happened after birth. Thus, women were neither superior nor inferior to men, there was no 'eternal feminine', and 'a woman has no special value because she is a woman. That would be the most retrograde "biologism", in total contradiction with everything I think' (M, 153). Women are not 'superior' to men for Luce Irigaray: 'why think in quantative terms? They are *different*' (I, 190).

For Suzanne Horer and Jeanne Socquet, there was no point in simply following what men have done. That would mean repeating the same mistakes:

> We must not follow in the footsteps men have imprinted on this earth. Why repeat the same errors with the same too obviously, catastrophic results? We do not believe in social revolutions that aim at "changing man". Such jolts shift problems without ever solving them in depth. (M, 243)

Hélène Cixous, though, rejected the idea of a 'general woman', or a single type of feminine sexuality (in "The Laugh of the Medusa"). She said there was no essence in femininity or masculinity, but that 'everything is language' (in V. Conley, 1984, 57). In *The Newly Born Woman* Cixous and Catherine Clément stated that there is 'no 'nature' or 'essence' as such', but, instead,

> living structures that are caught and sometimes rigidly set within historico-cultural limits so mixed up with the scene of History that for a long time it has been impossible (and it is still very difficult) to think or

even imagine an 'elsewhere'... (NBW, 83)

Appealing to the body is not necessarily essentialist, as feminists have noted (R. DuPlessis, 1985, 273; S. Gilbert, 1986, xvi; M. Hite, 1988, 123).

Donna C. Stanton has criticized Hélène Cixous' theories, seeing in them a return to the metaphysics of presence and identity, in which the technique of poetic metaphor suggests an economy of similitude, instead of one of difference (1986).

PART TWO

HÉLÈNE CIXOUS
THE *JOUISSANCE* OF WRITING

4

THE ECSTASY OF TEXTS

All the books that I could write revolve around the book that I shall never write, which allows all the others to be written, and this book of books is the book of You.

Hélène Cixous, "Preface" (C, xv)

There is only time to lose. Whoever believes there is lost time does not count themselves among the living. Nor amongst the dead: for the dead have only one longing, to come back alive…

Hélène Cixous, *La* (C, 65)

HÉLÈNE CIXOUS

Hélène Cixous is a stunning writer, so fluid, so powerful, so energetic, so erotic, so poetic. Her texts enmesh, so that diary merges into essay, lecture into philosophy, diatribe into pæan. Works such as *Inside, (With) Or the Art of Innocence* and *Extreme Fidelity* are wonderful.

> The mystery is that I do not understand the beings that I love the most [writes Hélène Cixous], and that even so that does not prevent me from either loving them or understanding them: what I do not understand is their own mystery, which not even they themselves reach. But I know their incomprehensibility well. (*(With) Ou l'art de l'innocence*, 1981, in C, 95)

Part of the *jouissance* of writing derives from needing to understand the other, to understand their language. 'For you are strange to me. In the effort to understand, I bring you back to me, compare you to me. I translate you in me' (Con, 146). The exchange that occurs in writing is thus like the exchange of lovers. 'The work we do is a work of love, comparable to the work of love that can take place between two human beings' (ibid.).

Hélène Cixous is one of the very few writers who possess a mastery (a mystery, a 'misstery') of language. She has the luminescence of Arthur Rimbaud, the deft control of language of Gertrude Stein or Samuel Beckett, and the *jouissance* of Sappho. 'Language englobes us and inspires us and launches us beyond ourselves, it is ours and we are its, it is our master and our mistress' (C, xix).

Hélène Cixous' range of writing is dazzling. Verena Conley writes:

> What sets her apart from other 'feminist' theoreticians – all of whom revalorize woman – is precisely that poetic *plus value* of pleasure she offers the reader as a gift in her writings. (1991, 126)

For Hélène Cixous, readers are crucial: as they read they write the text; they 'give rebirth' (DJ, 26), and writers need them. Despite the (apparent) essentialist theory in some of her mid-1970s texts, such as "Sorties" and "The Laugh of the Medusa", Cixous' works remain inspiring to many feminists.

There is no denying the sheer exuberance and polemical wit of "The Laugh of the Medusa". While feminists have argued about the exact meaning of Hélène Cixous' feminism in "Le rire de la Méduse", they have acknowledged the power of her poetic form of feminism. 'Poetic' is indeed the form Cixous' feminism often takes – it is a view of feminism and writing that privileges the intuitive, non-rational, non-masculinist and sensual response to the world. I do not think Cixous is best when she sticks to acerbic or polemical areas as some critics suggest (V. Conley, 1992, 131). I love it when she writes wildly and poetically. When she invents new imaginary spaces. A hyper-lyrical poetry. A new *Song of Songs.*

> I want vulva ...If the following words go out of my mouth, I will be able to see the two bodies in dull light, I will be able to traverse the Earth mixing with my living, my corporeal powers will not have any eclipse, eternally, and all she says is done from the point of view of my tongue: 'VULVA!' And out of the darkness where my divine, luminous mouth was vegetating a new star is being born. And I have my vulva! (*La*, 109-110, in V. Conley, 1992, 60)

It is at this point of wildness that Hélène Cixous can become problematical. Fine. Let her be problematical. One does not want a dead feminism that remains eternally in the dusty cloisters of academia. Cixous is not a writer or feminist who can easily be contained within one kind of ideology or feminist theory. Cixous' texts are very intense: they go to extremes all the time, always challenging established criteria, always questioning metaphysical and psychological limits. Cixous speaks in a truly Romantic vein when she admires extremism: 'I like all things extreme, it makes me discover things' (EHC, 176). Among the most explosive of Cixous' lyrical flights is the sustained pæan to Antony and Cleopatra at the end of "Sorties". Cixous rewrites Plutarch and William Shakespeare, showering lavish praise on the ancient Queen of Egypt, whom she calls 'inexhaustible', 'the enigma', who 'overfills without saturating', 'she is extravagance and abundance', 'surpasses the unsurpassable', 'unforgettable beauty', '[p]rofusion, energy, abundance' (NBW, 123-7). Cixous ends her fervent exaltation of Cleopatra with a portrayal of the orgasmic, mythic death of the lovers.

✤

In an interview, Hélène Cixous wonders (*pace* Clarice Lispector's *Agna Viva*) whether one can write (like) water, or read (like) water. The answer is to become 'one with the water' (EHC, 132). Cixous' artistic style is what she calls '*the style of live water*', a phrase which again echoes Lispector. Cixous' 'style of live water' is a style of flow and liquids.

> This style of live water gives rise to works which are like streams of blood or water, which are full of tears, full of drops of blood or tears transformed into stars. Made up of phrases which spill forth dripping, in luminous parataxis. (*Extreme Fidelity*, 25)

Hélène Cixous reckons that her form of feminine writing may have

> a more supple relation to property, which can stand separation and detachment, which signifies that it can also stand freedom – for instance, the other's freedom. (EHC, 137)

Hélène Cixous envisages texts that allow the other movement, freedom, not a text that limits itself. An edgeless text. Texts without boundaries. In *Illa*, Cixous writes of her key theme, departure:

> in accord with life, with body, we have to exit softly, leave all phrases of recommendation, and now live, simply live, live entirely there where we live, begin the way it begins. (137)

Cixous sees writing arising out of loss, disappearance, mourning. In her essay "De la scène de l'inconscient à la scène de l'Histoire: Chemin d'une écriture" ("From the Scene of the Unconscious to the Scene of History: Pathway of Writing"), she commented:

> In the beginning the gesture of writing is linked to the experience of

> disappearance, to the feeling of having lost the key to the world, of having been thrown outside. Of having suddenly acquired the precious sense of the rare, of the mortal. Of having urgently to regain the entrance, the breath, to keep the trace. (in F. Rossum-Guyon, 19)

The poetic project is thus the recreation of language, so that words become a compensation for loss. Writing is the recovery of life itself.

> Everything is lost except words... At a certain moment for the person who has lost everything, whether that is, moreover, a being or country, language become the country. One enters the country of languages. (ib., 19)

One sees this clearly in the efforts of love poets (Dante Alighieri, William Shakespeare, Sappho), where they try to recover and re-inhabit what was lost. The project of writing, then, is 'to leave this hell in direction towards the hidden day.' The goal is the present – being able to live in the present, to live the present: '[o]ne writes towards what is going to turn out at last to be the present. Paradise is that, it's managing to live the present' (ib., 9).

Writing is essential, Hélène Cixous says, but it does have limits. There is always the sneaking feeling, Cixous suspects, that writing is not enough on its own. 'And when I write I tell myself that it is not enough, we need to do something else' (*Extreme Fidelity*, 21). But when real sadness occurs close to the writer, writing loses its power, its limits become visible, the 'happiness in unhappiness' of writing is overcome by real suffering.

Oddly, Hélène Cixous says 'I think that I am constantly guilty... of having the privilege of being able to console myself poetically' (EHC, 140). A curious thought, which she instantly emends, by saying she that as she has consoled herself, she punishes herself. Cixous is clearly a writer who is never satisfied, who never reaches a still point, a quiesence, a point where she never needs to reach forward, to continue writing. Because she does continue to write; she is never still; she is never thoroughly consoled by poetry. Writing, for Cixous, is 'a consolation, happiness in unhappiness' (EHC, 141), a joy/ unjoy that exists in the present, but that crumbles as soon as real suffering is very near the writer. In the face of real suffering, writing soon reaches its limits.

✣

For Hélène Cixous, as for Andrea Dworkin, writing is an expensive way of living. That is, one must choose between living and writing. 'There are two writings; one writes books, the other writes living' (*Illa*, 207). *Pace* Franz Kafka, Cixous says

> Finally, writing chose him until he died. He paid, of course, with death. It is true that when somebody writes, somebody dies. It may be you. When you write, it may be only you. Kafka killed others, and then at a later moment he was the one who died. (EHC, 140)

Hélène Cixous wonders whether she is right to write. What right has she to write? To live, Cixous needs to write (one can say this was also true of Andrea Dworkin, Anaïs Nin, André Gide, John Cowper Powys, Henry Miller and Emily Dickinson, compulsive writers, writers who had to write to feel truly alive). Cixous says her need to write is 'totally unjustifiable, totally egotistical' (EHC, 142). She justifies herself, but she might be wrong. She knows this and continues to write.

> Cixous comes into life, is born, through writing. For her, to write *is* to live. Writing is always a question of life and death, a question that has its corrollary in another: who wants my death, who wants me to die? or, who wants me to live and love? (V. Conley, 1991, 14)

Hélène Cixous regards writing, like Andrea Dworkin, as essential to living: 'I need writing... I need writing to celebrate living'.[1] Cixous' texts are not traditional, not novels, essays, poems. Neither are they hybrids, like 'prose poems', or half-memoirs/ half-letters. They are self-contained, too. That is, for some critics, they are too self-referential, too involved in their own making and magic. Too much self-analytical 'I' and not enough historically sensitive 'we' or 'they'.[2] Instead, Cixous writes with her body – 'in', 'with', 'under', 'over', 'around' her body.[3] Cixous' excessive flows of words evoke the body, as nature, but it is also the body from which she writes (the cultural body). The body is therefore both the beloved object of writing, and the writing subject (F. Defromont, 120). The fluids of maternity and *jouissance* - milk, saliva, the juices of sex - are sensual metaphors of the economies of writing. As milk flows, so words flow. The titles of her works suggest movement, flight, opening, transgression, freedom: "At Circe's or the *Self-Opener*", "*Inside*", "The *Newly Born* Woman", "The *Exile* of James Joyce", "The *Laugh* of the Medusa", "Lemonade All Was So *Infinite*", "*Reaching* the Point of Wheat", "*Coming* to Writing", "*Three Steps* on the Ladder of Writing" (my emphasis). When she talks about sex, it is in terms of movements - some small, some subtle, some epic, some extraordinary. She talks about 'trips, crossings, trudges, abrupt and gradual awakenings' of erotic feelings (M, 256).

Many of Hélène Cixous' fictions are characterless, focussing instead upon some aspect of femininity, or fragments of a remembered past. In an early essay ("The Character of "Character"", 1974), Cixous had argued for taking characters out of fiction, as a way of subverting the marketing, coding and conformity of fiction. Occasionally men feature in the fiction, as fathers, brothers or lovers. However, in Cixous' plays men feature more prominently than women.

'I have to grow larger, stretch farther, want harder, be faster. I have to become gigantic. Exhausting!' (BP, 118). Desire erupts continually throughout *The Book of Promethea.* It is Hélène Cixous' most erotic text, where the *jouissance* of writing floods the words (even though nearly all her writing is suffused with sexual *jouissance*):

> I want your life. All I want is your life, nothing else. I want every drop of you. I want every thought. I want to drink your soul. Give me your soul to drink. (BP, 75)

In Hélène Cixous' poetics, desire undoes patriarchal dominance, it usurps absolutes, it destroys the singular 'I' of Western subjectivity. In *Prénoms de personne* Cixous defines desire as undoing the tyranny of death:

> I ask of writing what I ask of desire: that it have no relationship with the logic that puts desire on the side of possession, acquisition, consummation-consumption which, so gloriously pushed to the end, links (mis)knowledge with death. I do not think that writing – as production of desire, where desire is capable of everything – can be, or has to be, defined through the border of death. (1)

The sense of flux is one of Hélène Cixous' texts most conspicuous elements. Cixous' works do not keep still: her metaphors often concern fluidity, burning, metamorphosis. What Cixous promulgates is a sense of the self in the process of creation and transformation. As with poets such as Arthur Rimbaud, Cixous dislikes the fixed, that which cannot be overturned, or transformed. Her project (as with André Gide or Marcel Proust) is a quest of self-discovery, of self-creation and self-reflexivity. Like many poets from the Symbolist era onwards, Cixous enjoys observing herself as she creates. The texts become commentaries upon their construction. Sometimes the self-analysis involves a return to primal, maternal, œdipal spaces, sometimes it can read as embarrassing, arrogant, self-indulgent pleading.

Hélène Cixous' great strength is to make her lyrical, critical quest life-affirming, as well as entertaining and challenging. Like William Shakespeare and Giovanni Boccaccio, Cixous is a generous writer, big-hearted, full-blown, not a wimp given to snide, sarcastic remarks. In Cixous' work, writing (art) is a very important act of affirmation.

Unlike the Derridan project of founding a metaphysics of writing on absence and replacement, Hélène Cixous favours presence, and words as caresses. Cixous casts aside the notion of art based on 'lack' and goes for abundance. Like many poets before her, Cixous affirms the artistic act as a shamanic flight. Soaring, not scrabbling in the dirt; flying, not hopping up and down in one place and croaking the same tune (like politicians). In *Breaths,* the narrator bids women to soar. All manner of journeys. Imaginary journeys, real journeys; journeys of absence and of presence. One journey creates another: as one ends, another begins, because 'texts as desire 'make possible' what they desire by opening new spaces' (V.

Conley, 1992, 58).

In *The Newly Born Woman* and other texts, Hélène Cixous, at her most idealistic, advocates a poetics of transformation and transcendence, symbolized by a leap into the void or absolute. Like Existentialists such as Søren Kirkegaard, Cixous enshrines risk-taking and poetic leaps into the dark. Let's imagine, Cixous implores, 'a real liberation of sexuality', a 'transformation of each one's relationship to his or her body (and to the other body), an approximation to the vast, material, organic, sensuous universe that we are' (NBW, 83).

For Hélène Cixous, it is poets and writers and artists who are some of the people best positioned to make the leap and flight into the boundless. In their writing, poets may be able to make the spiritual flight into transcendence. In *Jours de l'an*, Cixous' narrator says:

> I defend my challenge as woman, my madness. I fly off, I land in the middle of a language. In a language you cannot die. Here the wind always blows, no word is immobile, the limit is not a limit.

In *Jours de l'an*, writing becomes another country, a space at once of the body and the spirit. The poet or artist is the one who can weave all this together. It is the act of writing that makes the connections, that binds these experiences together. Rainer Maria Rilke said the same thing.

Poets are not nationalistic, belonging to one nation, Hélène Cixous says; they are international. They are brought together by words, by writing, a circulation of letters.

> It is me, I, within the other, the other within me, it's one gender going into the other, one language going through the other, life through death

as Cixous wrote in *Difficult Joys* (14). Cixous knew that writing was special yet not at all special; that it was despised and repressed by authorities yet it has a secret influence; that authors have authority yet no authority at all (DJ, 28).

In her texts Hélène Cixous often weaves in allusions to the great names of world (i.e., mainly Eurocentric) literature. In *Le Livre de Promethea* Cixous folds in allusions to Dante Alighieri, Percy Shelley, Ludovico Ariosto, John Milton and the *Bible*, but, a critic maintains, is not tied down to this dominant culture because she keeps her distance via a technique of collage and allusion (M. Shiach, 1991, 100). In *Souffles* Cixous calls for a rewriting of classic texts such as the *Bible* from a feminine viewpoint. In "Castration or Decapitation" Cixous referred to classic tales such as the myths of Hera, Chinese women, and *Sleeping Beauty*; she saw in *Little Red Riding Hood* a metaphor of the clitoris, 'the female sex with her little jar of honey caught in a forest of male metaphors' (M. Humm, 1994, 108).

In *Le Livre de Promethea* Hélène Cixous took the classic myth of Prometheus and rewrote it: Prometheus became Promethea, much as Christ became Christa and Orpheus became Orphea in Monique Wittig's *The Lesbian Body.*

Hélène Cixous' intertextual journeys include encounters with James Joyce, Clarice Lispector, Franz Kafka, Torquato Tasso, Fyodor Dostoievsky, Jean Genet, Osip Mandelshtam, Paul Celan, Ingeborg Bachmann, Thomas Bernhard, Karen Blixen, Marina Tsvetaeva, Anna Akhmatova, Nelson Mandela, William Shakespeare, Lewis Carroll, E.T.A. Hoffmann, Friedrich Hölderlin, Heinrich von Kleist, Georges Bataille, Hugo von Hofmannsthal, Martin Heidegger, Sigmund Freud and Edgar Allan Poe.

In *First Names of No One* Hélène Cixous discusses Hoffmann, Joyce and Poe. In *Three Steps on the Ladder of Writing*, Cixous cites Kafka, Celan, Mandelstam, Bachmann, the Grimm brothers, Lispector, Dante, Hofmannsthal and Arthur Rimbaud. William Shakespeare was a constant source of inspiration – the 'being-of-a-thousand-beings', Cixous called him (NBW, 98).

Easy to see how a writer like James Joyce would fascinate Hélène Cixous: Joyce's mashing up of language was on an epic, determined scale. Instead of burning out in a short book, as Comte de Lautréamont and Arthur Rimbaud had done, Joyce kept up the momentum over a thousand or so pages. Joyce invented new poetries, which has always been one of

Cixous' main projects. In James Joyce's work the French Symbolists' insistence on musicality is given a thorough going-over. The early fictions are haunted by the voices of fictional lovers such as Heinrich von Kleist's Jeronimo and Count F., and Sigmund Freud's reworking of Wilhelm Jensen's *Gravida*. Cixous was attracted to Joyce's multi-level non-linear narrative, and the relation to subjectivity (Cixous, 1976). The creation of the artist also intrigued Cixous, the recognition in *Ulysses* and *Finnegans Wake* of the split artistic personality (P. Brooker, 1996, 286).

In Edgar Allan Poe's fiction Hélène Cixous saw the disruption of traditional representations of subjectivity via the cultivation of the unconscious (in *First Names of No One*). For Cixous, texts such as those of Jean Genet, Franz Kafka, Heinrich von Kleist and Clarice Lispector use economies that are 'open, expansive, generous, daring'. It doesn't matter that these texts are written by men or women. 'There are texts by men who are capable of other', as Cixous puts it in *Extreme Fidelity*. Poets are important for Cixous, because they cultivate the unconscious, that 'other country without boundaries... where the repressed survive - women or, as Hoffmann would say, fairies' (NBW, 98). The 'problem', rather, is with the women have had to masculinize their works 'in order to hoist themselves on to the scene of socio-political legitimation' (25).

For Hélène Cixous, writers 'write' each other. Thus, Marina Tsvetaeva 'wrote' Rainer Maria Rilke, and vice versa: '[s]he would ask Rilke, 'Write to me', or 'Write me my own letters'. It all works, as Rilke would say, as if there were only one poet. And this poet is a combination of many poets. Actually Rilke addressed a poem, dedicated a poem in three languages, to Tsvetaeva. He wrote it in German, he wrote in Russian and in French' (DJ, 17).

⚜

Do we need to discuss Hélène Cixous' essay "The Laugh of the Medusa" at length? - because it has been dealt with in detail admirably elsewhere.[4] However, it is foolish to ignore it completely, for it is probably Cixous' most widely quoted text, if not her most influential. Re-reading "Le rire de la Méduse" now, what is striking is the energy of the piece, its apocalyptical and transformative programme, its lyricism and commitment, as well as its infuriatingly simplistic sexism and interpretation of men, masculinity and patriarchy.

It must be recalled that Hélène Cixous' "Le rire de la Méduse" was published in 1975, in the midst of second wave feminism, in the same year as Laura Mulvey's influential essay "Visual Pleasure and Narrative" and Susan Brownmiller's *Against Our Will,* one year after Luce Irigaray's *Speculum* and Juliet Mitchell's *Psychoanalysis and Feminism,* one year after Simone de Beauvoir had founded Ligue Françoise pour le droit des femmes, five years after Kate Millett's *Sexual Politics,* Germaine Greer's *The Female Eunuch* and Shulamith Firestone's *The Dialectic of Sex,* and not long after Vietnam, Watergate and the embracing of Mao and Marxism by post-1968 intellectuals.

"Le rire de la Méduse" is couched in the polemical, harsh tone of anti-masculine second wave feminism, where the argument is distinctly framed in terms of 'us and them'. 'Them' was the enemy, men. Hélène Cixous' argument in "Le rire de la Méduse" is multi-layered and subtle, but it is also severely reductive and simplistic. Cixous reckons women are superior sexually, and in life in general. 'Woman', asserts Cixous, knows more than men about living, about desires and drives (M, 259). Such naïve generalizations are silly, but Cixous' project in "The Laugh of the Medusa" is founded on them.

Women, Hélène Cixous claims, do not fear risks, or desires, do not deny, nor hate, nor fetishize. They do not try to gain advantages over the other, they observe and sympathize/ empathize (M, 263). As with feminists such as Andrea Dworkin, Susan Brownmiller, and some radical lesbian feminists, Cixous regards men as responsible for many of the ills that women are suffering. Men, Cixous contends in "The Laugh of the Medusa", are responsible for many crimes against women, not least being their encouragement of the silencing of women, of leading women to hate themselves (M, 248).

Men have sidelined women's voices, Hélène Cixous asserts, a common complaint of second wave feminism. Women have been snared by silence.

Men haven't got it any easier, necessarily: while Cixous claims that there is hardly any writing that 'inscribes femininity' (248), '[m]en still have everything to say about their sexuality, and everything to write' (247). That is, though women have everything still to write, so have men. Men too have been deprived of their 'own bodily territory' (ib.).

Hélène Cixous is not, either, a man-hater, a common gripe made by men against feminists. No, Cixous' philosophy is about embracing everything, men included. Of course Cixous offers a place in her philosophy for men and their sexuality, including the penis. 'I want all', she says, 'I want all of me with all of him' (M, 262). For Cixous, life is about embracing everything, including the difficult, ambiguous, painful zones. Cixous says she does want the man, the whole man, and the whole woman, the whole person, 'whole and entire, male or female'. She wants it all because 'living means wanting everything that is, everything that lives, and wanting it alive' (ib.).

The problem of Lacanian lack and desire is depicted by Hélène Cixous in *Extreme Fidelity* of knowing what one has.

> There is a whole series of texts which work on the question of having, of *knowing how to have what one has*. It is one of the most difficult things in the world, since, poor humans that we are, no sooner do we have, than we no longer have... To have what we have is the key to happiness. In general, we have, we have a great deal, but because we have, we no longer know that we have. (21)

Thus, the trick is to

> remember at every moment what a blessing it is to have. To keep in the having the breathless lightness of hoping to have. To have just after not having had. To always have in us the emotion of having almost not had. For to have is always a miracle' (22)

Linked to Hélène Cixous' notion of knowing what one has is the idea of not really 'knowing'. That is, a kind of knowing that avoids being trapped by knowledge or comprehension, a knowing that incorporates understanding but does not blinker thought (ibid.). For Cixous, simply being alive is a kind of sainthood. Cixous is with Clarice Lispector, on the side of life, of saying yes, of accepting that living is good. 'All we need to do is to need and we have. Life is already there, always waiting for us'. Similarly, love is already there: '[i]t precedes us as the poem precedes the poet... It is the economy of thankfulness. All we need to do is to live and we have' (*Extreme Fidelity*, 24).

This is a world of hatred, Hélène Cixous says, where the selfish ego is primary, where people are more concerned with looking in the eyes of their peers than with really making contact. As Cixous point out:

> a phobia of nonidentity has spread, and individuals, and nations like individuals, are infected with this neurosis, this pain, this fear of non-recognition, where each constructs, erects, his auto-identification, less out of intimate recollection than out of a system of rejection and hatred.[5]

Hélène Cixous loathes the masculine view of sexuality that is found in culture, where sex is always associated with death. Men need women and femininity to be linked to death, Cixous said in "Sorties"; they need to fear women to get an erection (NBW, 69).

In *Prénoms de personne* (1974), Hélène Cixous analyzed the relations in masculinist poetics between sexuality, narcissism, identity and death. In the work of writers such as James Joyce and Edgar Allan Poe, Cixous saw that women were usually associated with death, a negative view which Cixous countered with her notion of the economy of the gift, which is linked to spending and loss.

For Hélène Cixous, the gift is one of women's key attributes, an embodiment of excess, abundance. The economy of the gift insists on relationality and exchange, on self and other, and how the economy of exchange relates to language and poetics. Instead of the Freudian economy of castration and its relation to the symbolic order and the law of the father, Cixous posits something else, 'a non-castrated subject, a non-phallomorphic language, *jouissance* (maternal giving) rather than ejaculation (economic reproduction)' (J. Still, 1993, 26). Instead of the masculine desire to appropriate and incorporate the other, the 'feminine economy' of the gift is based on mutuality and mingling (NBW, 85). The 'feminine' gift is a 'deconstructive space of pleasure and orgasmic interchange with the other', which Cixous gives a Derridean slant (T. Moi, 1985, 113). The feminine gift expects no profitable return, because 'woman' is 'never settling down, pouring out, going everywhere to the other' (NBW, 87).

While the 'feminine' libidinal economy is associated with the Realm of the Gift, the masculine economy is aligned with the Realm of the Proper: proper, property, appropriation, self-aggrandizement, colonialism, asserting dominance. Following Jacques Derrida, Mme Cixous posits a 'real gift, a pure gift, a gift that would not be annulled by what one could call a countergift', a gift that erases the giver, the 'I' or ego of the giver, makes the giver transparent; not an 'I-give', nor a gift that demands a 'thank you', because the 'thank you' implies debt, giving back part of the gift; rather, a gift like grace, but not a God-given gift (EHC, 158-9).

As they, men, approach Medusa, all they show, as Perseus, is their backs. They cannot face Medusa, the terrible reality of women, directly. They have to avert their gaze. Hélène Cixous scorns such cowardice. 'What lovely backs! Not another minute to lose. Let's get out of here' (M, 255). So much for the *heroic* Perseus. Oppressed, repressed, suppressed, women will break out, Cixous says. When the repressed (women) return, Cixous reckons, the result will be an 'explosive, *utterly* destructive staggering return'. After the rule of the Phallus is over, women will be 'annihilated or borne up to the highest and most violent incandescence' (M, 256).

This is the apocalyptic tone of "The Laugh of the Medusa", where nothing in-between extremes is considered, where the transformation will be into violent incandescence or nothingness. Either one or the other. No half measures. 'Don't open your gaze so wide for me. I am going to fling myself out of this gaze. Violence: everything is sweetness' (BP, 76).

Women are getting ready to break out, Hélène Cixous asserts. They have been muffled up for so long, living in their dreams and bodies, muted, in silence, fragile but also incredibly strong. The way back, the road to eruption, is via the body and writing, a writing of/ in/ through the body, an *écriture féminine* founded on the *jouissance* of the (female) body.

Here's where Hélène Cixous unsettles most feminists, but also where she is at her most utopian and idealistic. 'More body [than men], hence more writing' (257). Women's bodies, Cixous reckons, have been taken away from them.

Again, this is a common view in second wave feminism, in the feminisms of Robin Morgan, Susan Griffin, Andrea Dworkin and Annie Leclerc. Feminist rallies and conventions which aimed to 'take back the night' in the 1970s were partly about the reclamation of women's bodies. This was an initiative that bewildered the establishment, this radical politicization of the body. Was the body, then, also a political issue? Yes. So instead of being 'trapped' in their bodies, of having their bodies suppressed and oppressed, feminists spoke of liberating the body, of taking back the body from patriarchy. 'Touch me, caress me, you the living no-name, give me my self as myself' (252).

Hélène Cixous' project of creating a 'women's writing' in "Le rire de la Méduse", was more liberating and exhilarating than problematical, for it unleashed a discussion about the politicized female body, the body as text ('Text: my body' 257), the linked economies of eroticism, gender, art and ideology.

In *Tancredi Continues* Hélène Cixous writes of love as a flight, a yes or a no, with nothing in-between except the abyss which must be traversed by the flight of love. The 'movement of love', Cixous says,

> is a question of the grace of genders, instead of the law of genders, it is a question of dancing, of the aerial crossing of continents. It is a question in front of Jerusalem, *still only obscurely*, of the mystery of love which is a question of acrobatics: fly or fall! There are no detours, it is straight ahead. That is why it is so easy. Yes or No – there is no in-between. That is why loving is never difficult except in appearance. Because the opposite of 'easy' is not 'difficult': it is only *impossible*. (1988, 38)

The lover is thus the acrobat, leaping vertiginously across the abyss.

'We leap and there is grace' (ibid.). In her texts (in *La Jeune Née*, for example), Hélène Cixous plays with phrases such as *en vol* and *voler*, in flight, theft, and love spelt backwards (love/ *en vol*). They all point towards freedom, reflected in Cixous' free-form style of writing.

The early texts of Hélène Cixous, in the euphoria the French post-1968 era, were full of idealized visions: fictions such as *Dedans* (1969) and the trilogy *Troisième Corps, Les Commencements* and *Neutre* (1970-72), were written in and for an epoch where 'everything seemed possible' (E. Sartori, 68). These post-Marxian, post-Freudian expressions of second wave feminism becoming third wave (postmodern) feminism were part of the self-confidence that enabled the complexities and ambiguities of theory to be overridden by the utopian vision.

Hélène Cixous is incredibly optimistic, so utopian one wonders if she is going to explode under the pressure of her own evangelical exuberance. When she comes, Cixous claims, woman will be radically transformative, because she is 'vibrant', because her drives are 'prodigious', because 'she cannot fail', her libido will produce 'far more radical effects of political and social change than some might like to think' (252). It's all a poetry of extremes in "The Laugh of the Medusa", with Cixous claiming that women's eroticism is 'cosmic', and her unconscious is worldwide (259). No boundaries. Limitless. Vertiginous traversals of endless space. Women are 'stormy', and they are everywhere (248). Women's imaginary powers are infinite, Cixous asserts, they are fantastical and incredible (246).

> Nous, les précoces, nous les refoulées de la culture, les belles bouches barrées de bâillons, pollen, haleines coupées, nous les labyrinthes, les échelles, les espaces foulés; les volées, – nous sommes 'noires' *et* nous sommes belles.
> [We, the precocious, we the repressed of culture, our lovely mouths gagged with pollen, our wind knocked out of us, we the labyrinths, the ladders, the trampled spaces, the bevies – we are black *and* we are beautiful.][6]

Wow. It's breathless stuff, but also full of breath, of air, of wind, of being airborne, of flight. If Hélène Cixous is not using metaphors of shamanic flight and air, she speaks of burning and volcanoes. The new 'feminine text' will be 'volcanic', an upheaval: this is the language of the end of the world: smashing, shattering, breaking, blowing up (258). If things are so good for women, if they really do have 'cosmic' eroticism, a global unconscious, more body, no boundaries, what is stopping their revolution? What is holding them back? All sorts of things, but in a word: men. In more words: patriarchy and social systems.

Hélène Cixous' politicization and poeticization of the body is a bid to reclaim not only the body itself but its representation and operation in culture. Body and text become synonymous. Censoring the body becomes like censoring speech and art. In making art, then, one writes one's body, one's existence. 'Write your self: your body must be heard' (250). Women must get into the text, says Cixous (245). Their new, revolutionary writing will be 'the invention of a *new insurgency*', a new liberation (250).

The act of writing, Hélène Cixous claims, will 'realize' realms that have been suppressed, it will give back to women their goods, pleasures, organs, all the 'immense bodily territories' which have been buried by the establishment. Writing will be a tearing away of veils, a casting aside, an act of affirmation and seizing the time, an act of will and rights. '*Écriture féminine*' will have to occur to some extent *within* masculinist or patriarchal writing. Julia Kristeva also says this. If, however, the new 'women's writing' is going to operate within men's/ masculinist writing, it will have to use different tactics.

> ...it is time for her to dislocate this 'within,' to explode it, turn it around, and seize it: to make it hers, containing it, taking it in her own mouth, biting that tongue with her very own teeth to invent for herself a language to get inside of. (M, 257)

In "The Laugh of the Medusa" Hélène Cixous urges women to write, to create their desires, their bodies, their own worlds. It is a stream of imagination and invention. It is a culture of yearning, in which desire is the key, the engine, the motivator.

> I, too, overflow; my desires have invented new desires, my body knows unheard-of songs. Time and again I, too, have felt so full of luminous torrents that I could burst... (246)

This is why Arthur Rimbaud gave up poetry, because it could not sustain his own 'luminous torrents'. This is a problem that Hélène Cixous does not really address: that her own writing is marvellous, but that few women, or men, can write like her. In advocating a wild, torrential, bursting, desirous form of 'women's writing', Cixous does not acknowledge that this may be beyond the capability of some women, or men. Perhaps not every woman is capable of wild, shamanic flights of poetry. Perhaps she doesn't want the flight, anyway. Cixous does not give up: '[a]nd why don't you write? Write! Writing is for you, you are for you; your body is yours, take it', Cixous urges her reader (M, 246). And that means *you*, dear reader. Y-O-U.

Perhaps, some women might reply, my body is *already* mine; perhaps, writing or art is not the best means to transformation. Hélène Cixous offers her own explanation of why 'you', the reader, haven't written: because your efforts were secret, and not very good. You hide away, as when you masturbated in secret – this is the metaphor Cixous chooses: one's secret writing is like secret masturbation. An odd choice of analogy, but in keeping with Cixous' sexualization, feminization and poeticization of writing. 'The most beautiful things cannot be written, unfortunately. Fortunately' (BP, 53).

According to Hélène Cixous and many feminists, women have been silenced: but eventually the inner need to write becomes stronger than cultural silencing. In writing, women should remain in a critical relation to their languages and narratives. They should not adhere to the fixed categories of tradition. They should (try to) inhabit a space that is in-between inside and outside, an in-between space, the space of the 'third body'. In *Vivre l'orange*, Cixous' narrator speaks of living submerged under time, in a space below the ground. She talks of 'sojourning in inner Orient' (C, 88), a marvellous poetic combination of terms ('innerness' taken from psychology, and 'Orient' from the poetry of travel and exile, the Westerners' love of the East).

Writing, Hélène Cixous says in *Three Steps On the Ladder of Writing*, comes from 'deep inside', not outside; from the lower regions - from hell but 'it is of course a good, a desirable hell' (C, 203). Referring to Clarice Lispector's 'inferno' and Marina Tsvetayeva's abyss, Cixous says it is a place 'deep in my body, further down, behind thought' (C, 204).

For Hélène Cixous, writing is a form of Orphic descent and return - into the land of the dead, recalling the spiritual descents into the underworld of Isis, Jesus and Orpheus. 'Writing is a going to the realm of the dead, but we're not always aware of it' (DJ, 19). Writing makes one aware of mortality, of death, Cixous says. 'Writing is dying; it's being born and dying' (ib., 20). The poet has to descend, to the depths of the heart, the stomach, the womb; the mythic descent is

> more difficult to achieve, much more tiring, much more physically exacting... than climbing up. It is a climb, but it requires the whole strength of everything that is you. (C, 204)

✤

At times, Hélène Cixous sounds distinctly like the poet Rainer Maria Rilke, who said, in his *Sonnets of Orpheus*, that 'song is existence'. In *La venue à l'écriture*, Cixous writes in a Rilkean mode, making the links between speaking and being, between writing and the body:

> As if I were living in direct contact with writing, without interruption or relay. In me the son which, from the moment it's uttered, gains instant access to language: a flux immediately text. No break, sound-sense, sing-sound, bloodsong, everything's always already written, all the meanings are cast. (6)

In this book, Hélène Cixous relates the foundation of women's writing in the mother's body and voice. The first writing body (or body that writes) is the mother.

Hélène Cixous keeps going: don't stop, she says, let no one and nothing stop you: 'why don't you write? Write!' The endpoint of this command is the transcendence into shamanic, witchy flight. Feminist writers such as Sara Maitland and others have taken up the notion of flying women in feminist fairy tales. Towards the end of the extraordinary "The Laugh of the Medusa", Cixous writes:

> Flying is woman's gesture – flying in language and making it fly. We have all learned the art of flying and its numerous techniques; for centuries we've been able to possess anything only by flying; we've lived in flight, stealing away, finding when desired, narrow passageways, hidden cross-overs. (M, 260)

In "Sorties" Hélène Cixous, rewriting Heinrich von Kleist, speaks of love transforming bodies into

> a glorious radiant body, drawn toward summits, literally pushed headlong, *head up*. Vision of dazzling Assumptions, flights, self outdoing self... All of Kleist's work is a great field for taking off, for flying away in exultation. A field of passion; elation and pain, intricable joy and sorrow. A wreath of laurels and nettles. How I love it! (NBW, 113-4)

The Cixous-woman, then, is explicitly the witch or shaman, the angelic traveller to other worlds, the one who leaps into the abyss, who makes epic voyages or gradual awakenings, crossovers, transgressions.

> For her joyous benefits she is erogenous; she is the erotogeneity of the heterogeneous: airborne swimmer, in flight, she does not cling to herself; she is dispersible, prodigious, stunning, desirous and capable of others, of the other woman that she will be, of the other woman she isn't, of him, of you. (NBW, 89; M, 260)

It is Hélène Cixous who has written more passionately about writing than any other French feminist, or any other feminist. Cixous regards writing as the centre and foundation of her feminist project. She appears in her writings as one of those people wholly committed to writing, to the power and influence of it, to the necessity of it in everyday life. She appears in her texts as someone who cannot live or breathe without writing 'I cannot live without writing: and I cannot live without making love', Cixous writes in *Ou l'art de l'innocence* (279). Why does Cixous write about love? Because, she says in the preface to her *Hélène Cixous Reader*, love is at the centre of human experience:

> I see that in the poetic text, often or indeed always, I deal with love which is our fate, twisted thing, tortuous, delicate, eager, insatiable, the best and worst thing, the junction point between everything and nothing, the oxymoric knot of all existence, love which makes gods and cattle meat of us... (C, xxi)

When she writes, Hélène Cixous says in *Difficult Joys*, she writes with her body. 'I write very near my body and my pulsions' (DJ, 27). For Cixous, one is 'made by writing', by the texts one reads ('writing starts with reading'), texts become one's parents (DJ, 15). 'I have what I need. Land of my own, vast for exploring, working, surveying, leaving... I have enough fire for all my passions' (BP, 131).

Sometimes there is an erotic relation with a book, Hélène Cixous says: when one reads in bed, one is intimate with a text: '[y]ou feel the rhythm of the body, you feel the breathing and you make love with these texts' (DJ, 27). There can be 'a kind of carnal, fleshly, bodily relation with the book', in which readers might eat books, stroke books, books might give them orgasms or make them cry (DJ, 27). Cixous loves writing so much she speaks of the 'body of the text': she likes to work on texts that 'touch' her – literally. That is, physically. Cixous likes to examine texts as they look, typographically, word by word, working very closely with the text, as the body is close. Cixous believes in the 'bodily relationship between reader and text' (Con, 148).

In *La Venue à l'écriture*, Hélène Cixous writes:

> To write: making love to writing. To write through loving, to love through writing. Through writing, love opens the body without which writing shrinks. (52)

Cixous writes 'blind', using writing 'as surprise' (N. Ward-Jouve, 1991, 43). Cixous also writes, like André Gide, into a mirror, using writing as simultaneously the patient, the mirror and the psychoanalyst.

Hélène Cixous speaks of all writers (and all readers) being 'wounded by the coming of the text, being wounded by wonder because the joy that a text inflicts hurts' (DJ, 25). Writing and reading are likened by Cixous literally to food, to eating, sucking, kissing (CW, 19). Reading and writing are nourishment, *jouissance* and impregnation. Creativity is as essential to Cixous as food or sleep. She feeds off writing, and feeds writing back into her life at every level - the social, personal, sexual, political, ideological, historical, psychological, and poetic.

Hélène Cixous' writing thus moves between the personally historical (the quasi-autobiographical voice) and the traditionally historical (a quasi-objective voice). Cixous shifts from personal to social history. Cixous' project has thus embraced a number of issues and causes, from psychoanalysis and the liberation of the individual, to the legal system in France, Third World politics, the death camps, India, women's liberation, and so on.

In Hélène Cixous' poetic vision of writing, there is no division that can be made between writing and life. Outsiders cannot make this differentiation, but neither can the writing subject. It is Cixous who, again and again, reveals the exhilaration and the agony of the *jouissance* of writing. In *Lemonade tout était si infini,* Cixous' narrator speaks of 'writing with life. Life with writing' (C, 115). In writing, one can be as free as it is ever possible to become 'free'; simultaneously, one is never 'free' in writing, one is always imprisoned.

It is this double bind that Hélène Cixous explores in her open, soaring, pluralistic texts. Neither totally one thing nor the other. Not pure ecstasy without pure pain. Neither total certainty without total ambiguity. Fluidity is always enshrined. Has to be. No programme of writing (art) that is not fluid and always in motion could be tenable.

Thus, the Cixous-writer swoops from anguish to ecstasy and back again very swiftly, sometimes in the next sentence. A jubilant statement is immediately countered by a sober one. Thus, in *(With) Ou l'art de l'innocence*, one of her most powerful and personal texts, Hélène Cixous makes many statements that are central to her whole work ('I need writing... I write celebrating living', and so on), but immediately counters them, hedging them about with confusions, couching her declamatory statements with uncertain ones.

In *(With) Or the Art of Innocence*, Hélène Cixous explores the eternal triad of writer, text and audience; or, to put it another way, the triad of writer, you and love; or writing, loving and living; or desire, loss and desire. Always in Cixous' work there is an 'I' zooming through a panoply of emotions, an 'I' which is central, the 'I' of the poet, saying this, saying that. Cixous' 'I' is the artist's ego churning through the mixed and intense emotions of her everyday life. But this 'I' or self is always addressing another self, the 'you' of her writing.

In Hélène Cixous' writing, the audience or 'you' is always present. But this 'you' is mutable. Sometimes it is the 'you' as the lover, as in pop songs or the blues, which sing of 'missing you', 'wanting you'. This is the 'you' buried in the phrase 'I love you'. Sometimes it is the 'you' as a general public, or a 'you' which is a select coterie of the writer's acolytes. Or it is the 'you' that is the parents. Or the government or leading powers. Or the critics.

Often there is a feeling in Hélène Cixous' work that the 'you' is one particular person, someone the writer knows personally. Perhaps she was intimate once with this 'you', perhaps she desires to be intimate with her/him again. All the time in Cixous' work, and one can sense this too in Francesco Petrarch's *Canzoniere*, in Emily Dickinson's poems, in Sappho's fragments, there is a deep desire to really find and talk to and seduce the 'you' or object (subject) of the writing.

In *(With) Or the Art of Innocence*, Hélène Cixous grapples with writing 'the book of You' which can actually never be written. One might see James Joyce's vast *Ulysses* or the three hundred and sixty six sonnets and *canzone* of Petrarch's *Rime Sparse* as an attempt to circumscribe the eternal 'you'. The further and the more these writers write, the further away the

Grail becomes. It is a project, then, of eternal and continual failures. Oh, but what *beautiful* failures. This is what Cixous says: 'the most beautiful of all failures'.

There is a feeling that the writer, sitting back and surveying her/ his work, heaves a sigh and admits to failing, but also admits, well, this stuff is not half bad. In fact, at times, it's wonderful! Why not? One imagines Francesco Petrarch or Louise Labé or Gaspara Stampa putting down their pen and acknowledging the ultimate failure of their polished verses but also yielding to their delight in their work.

In *(With) Or the Art of Innocence*, Hélène Cixous asks many questions which simply put the writer's problem another way. Am I, she asks herself, transgressing by writing, and, if so, what am I transgressing? Do I transgress by *not* writing? Is writing automatically transgression? If so, I should know about it, consciously, shouldn't I?

Another series of questions revolves around (here we go again): what is writing *for*? Not for more writing, surely? Does the writer write simply in order to write some more, further, added, additional, surplus? Or is writing really to improve living? Is writing about making living richer? If so, is writing the best way of enriching life? Cixous says she writes to improve her reading, her body, her living.

Then the problem of the traditional highpoint of living in the West - loving - appears. In *(With) Or the Art of Innocence,* Hélène Cixous' narrator realizes that her writing is usually directed at something, and that something is usually a person, a thinking mind, a presence, and, further, that person/ presence is often a beloved, someone with whom the writer wishes to make deep contact. This is where more of the hell of writing comes. For the other, the beloved, the presence, brings with her or him ambiguity, doubt, confusion, pain.

Thus, Hélène Cixous in *(With) Ou l'art de l'innocence* acknowledges the failure of writing to 'you' even though she cannot stop herself ('I write to you, I write myself to you, I fail' [C, 100]). Later, Cixous' narrator-writer comes face to face with another of the writer's (artist's) eternal problems: solitude which turns into loneliness. There is no easy solution here, as anywhere in (Cixous' view of) art. Loneliness is loneliness, and won't go away. Writing, as many writers have realized, only partially dissolves loneliness. The imaginary becomes an insufficient companion. The anguish, as Cixous' narrator puts it in *(With) Ou l'art de l'innocence,* is experiencing life alone, not sharing it with a companion. As soon as the narrator gets to the 'regions of jubilation', she thinks of 'you'. Being there is not enough: she must have the companion. 'I cannot bear discovering all alone. I need you' (C, 104).

This is where anguish unleashes the fervour of the soul of the writer/ artist. On one side, the utter banality of mouthing 'I need you'; on the other, the terror of being alone. Is one going to shut up about one's pain? No. Because writing becomes an aid, a way, a quest of transcendence. The transcendence of going beyond needing 'you'. And then, to go beyond even oneself: 'I am writing to go beyond myself; but what anguish if I succeed' (C, 104).

Some critics see Hélène Cixous on a Dantean, mystical quest, with her texts traversing various hells, ending up in Eden, the state of innocence: art. The taste of fruit evoking the newness of childhood (in *(With) Ou l'art de l'innocence* and *Limonade tout était si infini*). The journey does not continue, as in the *Divine Comedy*, to Heaven, beyond Earth, but back to earthly life, to history (N. Ward-Jouve, 1990, 47). Cixous' texts begin with her questioning, which becomes the quest; questions such as 'who am I?' and 'who do I follow' ('Qui? Suis?') in *Illa* • 'your life, where now?', in *Anankè* • and 'where to live?', 'where are we?', in *Le Prénom de Dieu*. The human subject, whether in William Shakespeare or any other text, is always asking 'what is a human subject, what is it that makes us live so well and so badly…?' ("Preface", C, xvii).

Loneliness, absence, death, the abyss – isn't all this a little over-tragic, over-indulged, over-dramatic? Yes. But writing may be a way of pushing all of that stuff out of the way, leaving no room for it anymore. Writing may be, says Hélène Cixous in an essay "Coming to Writing" (1977), a 'way of leaving no space for death, of pushing back forgetfulness, or never letting oneself be surprised by the abyss' (CW, 4). In this view, writing is a way of taking back silence, stillness, stagnation and death. Writing may make good absence and nothingness; 'my voice repels death; my death; your death'.

This is a visionary view of writing, of writing as spiritual redemption. The ego of the artist assumes God-like portions: 'I write and you are not dead. The other is safe if I write' (CW, 4). Hélène Cixous writes inside death. Writing enables her to absorb the transformations into other states of being that death brings. For Cixous, writing is

> the key to death – with father or mother, with the sea, and transfiguration, with the transposition of dead parent into beautiful metaphor, with the becoming jewel signifiers of the dead person, with the economy of suffering and transformation of mourning into a strange joy – that's writing. Actually you write thanks to death, against death, beginning with death. (*Difficult Joys*, 19)

Pulling back from this abyss of loneliness and reaching the 'regions of jubilation' without an understanding, loving companion, Cixous-writer considers other ways of making contact with the beloved 'you'. One way, a technological way, is the telephone. And what an amazing device the telephone is, with its new-fangled illusion of presence. In the telephone, there is presence but not-presence, a not-presence which is not entirely absence. Here, humour comes to the rescue of the agonized writer:

> You say to me on the telephone: 'love and kisses'.
> And I, kissed, say: 'what an instrument the telephone is! What an angel!' And you in your body say: 'What a demon!' (C, 102)

In the telephone call, Hélène Cixous' narrator is not sure where absence ends and presence begins. The other is there and yet not there. Simple observations these, but they go to the quiddity of the artistic act, to life itself. After all, much of French feminism is founded on the really simple but powerfully felt emotions of the mirror phase, the semiotic and symbolic, the anal, oral, maternal, and so on. In the telephone call, Cixous sees a new take on the problems of the relationship between presence and absence, between the voice and the body, the voice and the individual. Cixous is by no means the first writer to discuss the disembodiment of the telephone and technology, the 'virtual reality' syndrome of computers and video and digital guff. But she is a poet who knows that one can communicate without telephones or speech. As she puts it:

> I like telephoning you from nearby without a telephone: closing my eyes is all I need to do. One telephones best at night, of course, when the whole world has closed its eyes. (C, 102)

Hélène Cixous' texts veer from the optimistic to the cataclysmic. Often a 'positive' work is followed by something less optimistic. *La* is one of Cixous' most life-affirming texts. The project in *La* - of flying, climbing, escaping from the underworld of the repressed - is accomplished in an imaginary yet-to-be-realized future:

> Sans ailes s'éloigner du perchoir, sans l'angoisse, avec elles, passer avec ses âmes, ses former et toutes ses lettres à l'infini où elle prendra son là. [To move away from the perch without wings, without the anguish, with the women, to go with her souls, her forms and all her letters into the feminine infinite where she will take her.] (*La*, 278)

Immediacy and spontaneity are important to Hélène Cixous. In an essay, "Le dernier tableau ou le portrait de Dieu", Cixous expresses her desire to write like a painter (she refers to Post-Impressionists such as Vincent van Gogh and Claude Monet),[7] to be able to capture the changing present moment, the 'quasicles' ('quasi-miracle-instants') which she describes in *With ou l'art de l'innocence* (142).

Hélène Cixous talks about 'the other side' ('l'autre côté'), a metaphor of space which recurs in Cixous' writing (she speaks of the Kingdom of the Dead in *La*, and to Lewis Carroll's *Through the Looking Glass*). In *Illa*, Cixous writes in her idealistic mode of presence and naming:

> All the names of everything that grows sing her too, accompany her. In their basket, the delicious immensity of distance full of presence, to go

> away without leaving each other, the space in them, like the depth of proximity, the flesh of their flesh, the earth become tenderness. (23)

In *Vivre l'orange/ To Live the Orange*, a bilingual text (Hélène Cixous worked on the English translation), a series of explorations on sensuality (touch, smell, taste, sight), birth, motherhood, time, memory and selfhood cluster around the image and metaphor of the fruit. The emphasis is on (*pace* Clarice Lispector) flow and alterity, embodied in the fruit's juice. In *Vivre l'orange*, Cixous writes at her most lyrical, writing of touches of 'infinite delicateness', 'the benediction of the fruit', 'the juice-filled fruits of meditation', 'slowness which is the essence of tenderness' and the instant or moment which 'breathes, deepens, comes and goes, approaches, waits, continually' (C, 84-88). *To Live the Orange* is one of the Cixous texts where she really lets go, as with *The Book of Promethea* and *(With) Or the Art of Innocence*, where practically every sentence is heavy with poetry.

> Out of love for infinite delicateness of their voices. Out of respect for the delicateness of the nearness. Those whose speaking is so profound, so intense, whose voices pass gently behind things and lift them and gently bathe them, and take their the words in their hands and lay them with infinite delicateness close by things, to call them and lull them without pulling them and rushing. (C, 84)

5

HÉLÈNE CIXOUS AND ARTHUR RIMBAUD

not a single word ever returns from the luminous depths where our truth lives. The few words that come close are turned into sighs – so, the truth which only lives sheltered by silence, is forced to appear, and then she is like a fish out of water, thinking in a final convulsion of the sea, then, the end.

Hélène Cixous, *Tancredi Continues* (S. Sellers, 1988, 50)

HÉLÈNE CIXOUS, ARTHUR RIMBAUD AND THE FLIGHT OF POETS

> *One cannot bear to spend a Season in Paradise without crying out in instant nostalgia: never will we have the strength to endure such intoxicating agony a second time. If we had what we will never have – time to live this day over again – there are so many others desirable and each is the most beautiful one. It is superhuman torture. We do not know how, simply, to bear it. We weep for joy.*
>
> Hélène Cixous, *The Book of Promethea* (86)

Hélène Cixous has developed a way of writing which has affinities with what Arthur Rimbaud (1854-1891) might be writing if he were alive today. This may be a stupid thing to say, in a way, but Cixous' texts have that fluidity, that inter-changeability, that mordant wit, that *jouissance,* and that luminescence which one associates with Rimbaud's poetry. Like Rimbaud's poetry, Cixous' writing moves from being poetry to prose, weaving in elements of essays, lectures, speeches, diatribes, diaries and criticism. What Cixous has to say about writing fits so well with what Rimbaud said of the otherness of writing, the creation of self:

> Writing is the passageway, the entrance, the exit, the dwelling place of the other in me – the other that I am and am not, that I don't know how to be, but that I feel passing, that makes me live – that tears me apart, disturbs me, changes me, who? (1986, 86)

This fits in with Arthur Rimbaud's writing about the self/ not-self complex, the 'I' that actually is 'an other' ('je est un autre'). In another place, Hélène Cixous writes:

> Pure I, identical to I-self, does not exist. I is always in difference. I is the open set of the trances of an I by definition changing, mobile, because living-speaking-thinking-dreaming. (C, xviii).

For Hélène Cixous, Arthur Rimbaud's poetry is dominated by the authorial 'I', the narcissistic self. This is understandable in a poet just beginning to work:

> When one begins to write, one is constantly reminding oneself of the fact: 'I write'. Rimbaud is a good example, his verse echoes with 'I', 'I', 'I' ...an absolutely magnificent, exploded 'I'. (Con, 153)

Hélène Cixous writes of the self in a Rimbaudian fashion:

> I'll tell you frankly that I haven't the faintest idea who I am, but at least I know I don't know. I am not the other able to perceive me. I know some things about myself. I know who I'm not, I believe. (*Three Steps on the Ladder of Writing*, 51)

It's this 'absolute passion' that many poets and writers love about Arthur Rimbaud. His act of writing went to extremes. His extremism had a terrifying purity about it. Poets such as Rimbaud, Friedrich Hölderlin and Sappho burned brighter than most. Andrea Dworkin, like Hélène Cixous and Julia Kristeva (although her politics and feminist theory is very different from Cixous' or Kristeva's), looks also to Jean Genet or Franz Kafka, writers who expose the brutalities of the system. Clearly, for feminists such as Cixous, Kristeva and Dworkin, Rimbaud is an inspiration. Beyond the apparent misogyny, duality and gender confusion of some of the poems, these feminists appreciate the fierce ontological struggle of Rimbaud. Rimbaud may have written some harmful or stupid things about women, but he is immensely inspiring even so.

The elevating of male writers, though, is a problem for Anglo-American feminists, who have tirelessly enshrined women writers – the famous ones (Emily Brontë, Jane Austen, Angela Carter, Alice Walker, Adrienne Rich) and the neglected ones. Anglo-American feminism emphasizes the (biologically) female writer, and the (biologically) female reader. This is a strategy of reclaiming the past, past writers, past art. French feminists are not so concerned with the past, with exhuming and extolling in a polemical crusade; rather, they are very much rooted in the present, and the immediate future. Always French feminists stress what is happening *now*. To the body, in culture, in society.

Arthur Rimbaud - and Charles Baudelaire, Francesco Petrarch, Emily Dickinson, William Shakespeare - could have written: 'I have always loved desire'.[1] Like Rimbaud, Hélène Cixous advocated a culture of desire that was not founded on possession. Their form of desire came from being light-footed, from travelling light, not being weighed down by the obsession to possess. A culture of poetry which remains free at its metaphysical foundation. Never *me*, because 'I is another', because something speaks through me, something *speaks me*.

> I ask of writing what I ask of desire: that it have no relation to the logical which puts desire on the side of possession, of acquisition, or even of that consumption - consummation which, when pushed to its limits with such exultation, links (false) consciousness with death. (C, 27)

In French feminism a text can be 'feminine' regardless of who creates it. For Hélène Cixous a man can write a 'feminine' text (such as Jean Genet). Just because it is impossible to define a 'feminine practice of writing', though, does not mean that it does not exist, says Cixous (M, 253). It is easier to say what *'écriture féminine'* is not than what it *is*. It will be a practice or discourse that goes beyond the phallocentric system. It is the poets, Cixous claims, that are the ones who create *'écriture féminine'*, because they are in tune with the unconscious, like witches or shamans (M, 250). Poets, like women, have access to the 'other limitless country' of the unconscious, which is 'the place where the repressed manage to survive' (ib.). Poets are 'yes' people, life-affirmers, who say 'yes' to life (M, 255).

Arthur Rimbaud's poetry moves towards the 'feminine', rejoicing in evoking the pleasure (*jouissance*) of the text. Rimbaud goes ahead and writes that 'feminine' text which Hélène Cixous talks about. Other poets who have written in that 'outsider', 'feminine' fashion would include Sappho definitely, and Rainer Maria Rilke, and I would widen the scope to include poets such as Emily Dickinson, Louise Labé, Anna Akhmatova,

Osip Mandelstam, Marina Tsvetayeva, Paul Valéry, maybe Verlaine and Mallarmé, Baudelaire and Keats.

Hélène Cixous' range of poets that are to be exalted is slim – like Julia Kristeva, she refers to James Joyce, and Clarice Lispector. In *Three Steps on the Ladder of Writing*, Cixous mentions Franz Kafka, Paul Celan, Osip Mandelstam, the Grimm brothers, Clarice Lispector, Dante Alighieri, Hugo von Hofmannsthal and Arthur Rimbaud. Many of Cixous' preferred or referred to writers are outsider types, on the margins of society, feeling alienated (Fyodor Dostoievsky, Franz Kafka, Jean Genet, Anna Akhmatova, Arthur Rimbaud), or they are intensely lyrical (Dante Alighieri, Arthur Rimbaud, Friedrich Hölderlin, Clarice Lispector).

Julia Kristeva in (*La Révolution du langage poétique*) brings in writers such as Antonin Artaud, James Joyce, Comte de Lautréamont, Ferdinand Céline and Stéphane Mallarmé. These are (mainly European) writers, Kristeva reckons, who dissolve boundaries between identities, whose writing evokes fluidity.

The writers Julia Kristeva and Hélène Cixous allude to are all tried and trusted big names of the literary world. Writers such as Joyce and Dante, for example, have vast scholarly universes built up around them, which are being expanded all the time. Every year hosts of new articles, monographs, reviews and deluxe collector's edition clothbound books are published on Dante, Joyce, Shakespeare, Rimbaud and Dostoievsky.

There are no airport fiction or pulp novelists, or 'popular' blockbuster writers in the Kristeva-Cixous pantheon, no Jackie Collins, Dean Koontz, Tom Clancy, John Grisham, Dan Brown, Stephen King, etc. All their beloved writers are of the trendy, *avant garde* sort. They are also mainly male (Lautréamont, Artaud, Joyce, Céline, Rimbaud). Cixous and Kristeva (and, to a lesser extent, Luce Irigaray) are not bothered by enshrining male writers.

This elevating of male writers, though, is a problem for Anglo-American feminists, who have tirelessly enshrined women writers – the famous ones (Emily Brontë, Jane Austen, Angela Carter, Alice Walker, Adrienne Rich) and the neglected ones. Anglo-American feminism emphasizes the (biologically) 'female' writer, and the (biologically) 'female' reader. This is a strategy of reclaiming the past, past writers, past art. French feminists are not so much concerned with the past, with exhuming and extolling in a polemical crusade. Rather, they are very much rooted in the present, and the immediate future. Always French feminists stress what is happening *now*. To the body, in culture, in society.

Hélène Cixous writes of a writing which is desperate, which risks the really important things in life, which the writer needs to write in order to keep alive.

> I need writing [Rimbaud did too, for a while]; I need to surprise myself living [Rimbaud demanded this of poetry, but it couldn't deliver]: I need to feel myself quiver with living [think of Rimbaud's 'deschooling' of the senses]: I need to call myself into living and to answer myself by living: I need to be living in the present of the present [Rimbaud knew this was the only place to live]: I need double-living: I need to come into life [this was Rimbaud's aim in his disaffected teenage]: I am afraid that writing will take the place of living [Rimbaud, realizing this problem, jettisoned writing]: I need writing thinking of living; I wrote celebrating living [Rimbaud's poetry is always celebration] (*(With) Ou l'art de l'innocence* [*(With) Or the art of innocence*], 1981, in C, 95)

This is pure Rimbaud, more of Rimbaud than Rimbaud himself. And of course Rimbaud *did* follow this ancient command of freeing oneself from every kind of shackle. His project was indeed to destroy all shackles, ties, ropes, laws, rules, boundaries, limits, dogmas, doctrines.

Hélène Cixous, in *Three Steps on the Ladder of Writing* (1993), writes eloquently of the poetic act, and likens it to movement, in particular walking, and sex – the body in action:

> Walking, dancing, pleasure: these accompany the poetic act. I wonder what kind of poet doesn't wear out their shoes, writes with their head. The true poet is a reveller. Poetry is about travelling on foot and all its substitutes, all forms of transportation.

The poet, reckons Hélène Cixous, creates in motion, writes as s/he moves, moves as s/he writes. Creation, dreaming, movement and art are entwined.

> So perhaps dreaming and writing do have to do with traversing the forest, journeying through the world, using all the available means of transport, using your own body as a form of transport.

Hélène Cixous goes on to speak of Hugo von Hofmannsthal's book *The Wanderer,* in which the narrator meets a strange traveller:

> This man has apparently been walking for centuries, he is never named, but when you have lived in the country of poets, you immediately recognize who he is: he is Rimbaud. To meet Rimbaud we have to walk to Austria, to the Greece that is hidden within Austria; we have to travel to the heart of the country of the unconscious, where we may again find those countries we have lost, including Algeria and the Jardin d'Essais. But for this we have to walk, to use our whole body to enable the world to become flesh, exactly as this happens in our dreams. In dreams and writing our body is alive: we either use the whole of it or, depending on the dream, a part. We must embark on body-to-body journeys in order to discover the body. (1993, 64-65)

Hélène Cixous adds, in a statement, that

> In order to go to the School of Dreams, something must be displaced, starting with the bed. One has to get going. This is what writing is, starting off. It has to do with activity and passivity. This does not mean one will get there. Writing is not arriving; most of the time it's *not arriving*. One must go on foot, with the body. One has to go away, leave the self. How far must one not arrive in order to write, how far must one wander and wear out and have pleasure? One must walk as far as the night. One's own night. Walking through the self toward the dark. (ib.)

The affinities between Hélène Cixous and Arthur Rimbaud deepen the more one reads both writers. How close to Rimbaud's sensibility is Cixous' orgasmic, vertiginous writing:

> I think that one transgresses (1) the law of silence that must be observed

> in the face of everything that is bigger, more real, more living, more complex etc., in the face of almost everything. (*(With) Ou l'art de l'innocence,* in C, 95)

What Arthur Rimbaud came to realize, like so many poets (T.S. Eliot, William Shakespeare, Lawrence Durrell), is the limitation of words, of poetry. What Rimbaud was searching for, like writers such as Anaïs Nin and Rainer Maria Rilke, was a way of making art that would be like life itself, so the two were one. As Hélène Cixous writes in *Jours de l'an*:

> Get rid of the words that separate us from the world, and that cry out their fear, and that are made to dissuade us from reaching and leaving, and from touching and going beyond and tasting everything promised us in the world... (1990, in C, 183)

RAINER MARIA RILKE.

Hélène Cixous writes of Rainer Maria Rilke's Orpheus poems (*Sonnets To Orpheus*, 1926) as an example of the classic urge to dominance of masculine economy. Critic Verena A. Conley explains Cixous' position:

> In Rilke's poem to Eurydice she [Cixous] disengages what she calls the classic masculine structure of the poet who calls his (absent) beloved and makes her even more absent through the literal dispersion of her name: E, I. Eurydice dismembered is behind Orpheus. Always already lost, she *is* at the locus of separation without possibility for reparation. Melancholia, mourning, detachment are masculine attributes. Woman as life-givers stress the continuum. (V. Conley, 1991, 101)

For Hélène Cixous, Rainer Maria Rilke did not produce theory; rather, 'with the peculiar instrument infinitely freer than philosophical discourse, [he] produced a series of works that are living objects in which you see, for example, how a rose opens up' (EHC, 1991, 152). Cixous' open, lyrical prose, such as in *The Book of Promethea* and *(With) Or the Art of Innocence*, has affinities with Rilke's poetic style in *Sonnets to Orpheus*; an open, elegant, flowing and at times ecstatic kind of writing. The poetic thinking of Cixous and Rilke chimes at many points. For example, in Cixous' insistence on living fully in the present moment, one of the main themes of the *Sonnets to Orpheus*. Also, the relation between poetry and life, encapsulated in Rilke's Orphic phrase *dasein ist gesang* ('song is existence'); that is, singing (poetry, creativity) is life. Like D.H. Lawrence, Rilke advocated a mode of being fully alive, but, like Cixous, acknowledged how difficult it was to achieve in actuality.

In Rainer Maria Rilke's *œuvre,* the most celebrated manifestation of the Goddess or divine feminine presence is undoubtedly in the poem Hélene Cixous refers to, 'Orpheus. Eurydice. Hermes', one of Rilke's key works. This focuses on the mystery and solitude of the Goddess:

> She was deep within herself, like a woman heavy with child, and did not see the man in front, nor of the road ascending into life, withdrawn within herself; filled to the brim with that great fullness of her heaving died. Full as a fruit with sweetness and with darkness her groat death filled her; and it was so new, that comprehension failed her utterly. She into a new virginity and was untouchable; her sex was closed like a young flower at nightfall; her hands, so unused to marriage rites, felt the light god's gentle and guiding touch repellent, as too intimate and close. (1987, 51-53)

The poem 'Orpheus. Eurydice. Hermes' is 95 lines long, with Eurydice's entrance occurring at the halfway mark (between the 46th and 47th lines). Both Eurydice and Orpheus are given 26 lines of the poem. Elizabeth Sewell notes the 'sudden leap in power, intensity, sympathy' when Eurydice makes her entrance 'softly but emphatically' (1961, 328-30). The poet identifies with the figure of the woman, and makes a 'long, loving, cherishing, utter rejection of sex and fertility' (ib., 330). What Rilke's Eurydice embodies is not being pregnant with life, but with death: she is bearing the fruit of 'the Open'. Rilke's narrator in 'Orpheus. Eurydice. Hermes' takes Eurydice back, to the plant: 'first fruit, then flower, finally, as a culmination, root, as if to take her back, away from fruition into the earth, in the grace' (ibid.).

FRIEDRICH HÖLDERLIN.

Another German poet who has affinities with Hélène Cixous' poetic style, along with Rainer Maria Rilke and her beloved Heinrich von Kleist, is Friedrich Hölderlin. Hölderlin's poetry is not soft and gentle: it has more than a few thunder storms and flashes of lightning, like much of Romantic poetry. The atmospheres of the snowy Alps, the winds of a mythic, remembered Greece, and the wild woods of ancient Germany form the sensual foundation of Hölderlin's poetry.

The series of hymns and odes of the 1790s and early 1800s, the era of *Hyperion* and Friedrich Hölderlin's Hellenic enthusiasm, are extraordinary: 'Exhortation', 'Der Nekar', 'To the Germans', 'The German's Song', 'The Poet's Vocation', 'Return to the Homeland', 'Sung Beneath the Alps', 'Her Recovery' 'Go down, then, lovely sun', 'Palinode' and 'Hyperions Schiksaalslied' ('Hyperion's Song of Fate').

'Hyperion's Song of Fate' is one of the best examples of Friedrich Hölderlin's lyricism, his Orphic/ shamanic voice, his Hellenism, and his triumphant use of the hymn or ode form. Many of the odes and hymns are energetic invocations to the gods (such as Vulcan), to the ancient Greeks or modern day Germans, to Nature, or Mother Earth, or notions such as Peace, Hope, the Homeland, Love, those personifications which require a capital letter. 'And what else? Everything unsayable: laughter. Our cosmic mental geography. Our joyful megalomania, our coronations, our dates with the gods' (BP, 111).

Are there still gods? Hélène Cixous, in her own way, acknowledges the gods. Referring to William Shakespeare, the Renaissance and the theatre, Cixous says there have always been gods (especially in the theatre, in art); the gods are superior powers that interfere in human affairs, that mock humans; but 'the gods themselves are part of us'. Now they have modern names, 'pulsions, "drives", the id, laws, order and disorder, the paradoxical instance... structure' ("Preface [C, xix]).

Hélène Cixous refers to the key tenet of Renaissance magic and alchemy, 'as above so below': the gods are all that is in people but also stronger than them, over-vaulting them; 'and let us add: as below so above, no below without above etc' (ibid.).

Friedrich Hölderlin, like Hélène Cixous, Arthur Rimbaud and Rainer Maria Rilke, had an exalted view of the poet; they believed in the notion of the poet as shaman, a *sacer vates* or *poeta theologus*, a prophet, the high priest of people, more William Blake than William Wordsworth.[2] Hölderlin related the *sacer vates* to poets such as Pierre Ronsard, Sir Philip Sidney, Friedrich Gottlieb Vida, John Milton, Marco Klopstock and Torquato Tasso (ib., 11). As he wrote in 'An die Deutschen' ('To the Germans'), 'sweet it is to divine, but an affliction too' (F. Hölderlin, 1994, 117). Hölderlin also wrote of the poet as a hero, someone potentially titanic, whom Hölderlin compared to Achilles and Hercules. On the one hand, Hölderlin exalted the power and stature of the hero figure; on the other hand, he recognized that humility was crucial.

Friedrich Hölderlin is a 'poet's poet', in the sense that he creates 'pure poetry', poetry which does not require footnotes or explications, poetry which comes from individual feeling and thought, poetry which, though it is a product of its time and fashion, as all art is, strikes out of its own, carving its own niche in the cultural fabric of the West, poetry which builds on pure lyricism, poetry which, despite his later madness, remains passionate and authentic, imbued with the authenticity of the artist creating at the height of his /her powers. Hölderlin's free rhythms were 'so easy and poised, the pattern so subtle, that the art is unobtrusive', wrote Ronald Peacock.[3] Like Rainer Maria Rilke, Arthur Rimbaud, Marina Tsvetayeva, Heinrich von Kleist, Paul Valéry and Friedrich Hölderlin, Cixous also writes in a kind of 'pure' form, a lyrical kind of prose that transcends its era and context, a poetry that moves towards the universal, with its evocations of simple but also enduring things, such as apples, trees, the sky and the sea. As with Hölderlin, Rilke, Kleist, Valéry, Tsvetaeva and Rimbaud, Cixous' writing also deals with abstractions and personifications that have been part of poetry for millennia (abstract concepts such as 'Love', 'Time', 'Truth', 'Life' and 'Death').

Like the self-confident poet, Hélène Cixous' narrator in *Jours de l'an* knows s/he is powerful ('I had the power... I have the unknown power of myself, which is nakedness. I dive' [C, 184]). This is the voice also of Arthur Rimbaud in *A Season in Hell*, the voice of an artist feeling inflated, powerful.

Hélène Cixous speaks of literary texts which deal with 'libidinal education'. This bears directly on Arthur Rimbaud's poetry, which, from 'Seven Year-old Poets' through 'Memoire' and 'The Drunken Boat' to the mature work, *A Season in Hell*:

> We have worked on a group of texts which belong to what can be called the literature of apprenticeship, the *Bildungsroman*, and all of the texts – and there are a lot of them because literature is after all their domain – which relate the development of an individual, their story, the story of their soul, the story of their discovery of the world, of its joys and its prohibitions, its joys and its laws, always on the trail of the first story of all human stories, the story of *Eve and the Apple*. World literature abounds in texts of libidinal education, because every writer, every artist, is brought at one moment or another to work on the genesis of his/ her own artistic being. It is the supreme text, the one written through a turning back to the place where one plays to win or lose life. (*Extreme Fidelity*, C, 132)

The trouble is, as soon as the apple of life is grasped, the laws and prohibitions come into operation. As Hélène Cixous puts it: '[t]here is an apple, and straight away there is the law' (C, 133). With the apple comes the law: Eve (woman) is punished, Cixous says, because she has access to the inside, to pleasure, to touching. Eve

> is punished since she has access to pleasure, of course a positive relationship to the inside is something which threatens society and which must be controlled. That is where the series of "you-shall-not-enter" begins. (C, 134)

The fruit is the return of the state of innocence: Eden: i.e., the joy of writing = the joy of childhood. Childhood = innocence = writing = joy. Most works of literature graphically explore the desire and the prohibition, the lust for life and the laws that come down like walls of steel around the soul. One sees this agony of desire and fear so clearly in Arthur Rimbaud's *Illuminations* and *A Season in Hell*. Rimbaud's poetry is all about reaching for the apple, then grasping it, then exploring its richness. Cixous uses the metaphor of the *inside* of the apple, and this notion of interiority has particular resonance for poets such as Rimbaud, and Rainer Maria Rilke, who spoke of the insides of fruit expanding in the mouth. As Rilke poeticizes in his *Sonnets To Orpheus*:

> But glean the knowledge on a child's rapt face when he tastes fruit. This comes from heavenwards. Is something wordless growing in your mouth? Freed from the fruit's flesh, lightly as your breath, things found will fill your mouth, not common words. (1991, 13)

This fruitful expansion in the mouth activates various planes, including the erotic, the poetic, the linguistic, the synæsthetic and the religious. Rainer Maria Rilke connects tasting (the body) and speaking (language, poetry), speaking and Orphic song, the Orphic song as a cosmic rejuvenation: heaven growing in your mouth. In Rilke's poetics, the revolution in the body and the senses mirrors the religious and mythic revolution. Macro and microcosms merge (it is the 'above, as below' tenet of hermeticism and magic).

> It is the struggle between presence and absence [writes Cixous in *Extreme Fidelity*], between an undesirable, unverifiable, indecisive absence, and a presence, a presence which is not only a presence: the apple is visible and it can be held up to the mouth, it is full, it has an *inside*. And what Eve will discover in her relationship to simple reality, is the inside of the apple, and that this inside is good. (C, 132)

Arthur Rimbaud, of course, was very concerned with going beyond the laws and boundaries of his psycho-social context. He was a poet who instinctively and conscientiously broke boundaries. He explored the edges of art, and mused how he could go over the edge. In *The Newly Born Woman*, Hélène Cixous writes that intention and desire are patriarchal: '[i]ntention: desire, authority – examine them and you are led right back...to the father'. So that '[e]ither woman is passive or she does not exist. What is left of her is unthinkable, unthought' (C, 39).

Hélène Cixous writes in the Rimbaudian manner of wildness and outrage in *La* (*The [Feminine]*) published in 1976. Cixous conjures up a female/ feminine writing which is powerful and intoxicating. To reach this state of 'feminine writing' requires ample doses of *jouissance*, Cixous, as ever, proves herself to be more than capable of delivering *jouissance* plus *jouissance*:

> Show
> Her art of living, her abysses, of loving them, of making them sing, change, resounding their air with the rhythms of her earth tongues, regardless of the littoral and acoustic delimitations of their syllabuses.
> Her art of crossing the whole of history and its little histories and the contests of the sexes, and of crossing unscathed the foul economies, in a spirited stroke,
> from her inexhaustible source of humour
> [...] She knows not no, name, negativity.
> [...] She is simultaneously her animals of joy, her artists, her reasoning beings, her animals of prey, her aggressive souls, her love persons. (C, 59-60)

Whether or not this sort of scalding writing is 'Rimbaudian' is a question that might require more exploration. Is Cixous Rimbaudian, or is Rimbaud Cixousian: discuss in not less than 40,000 words. Yes. Cixous' form of free-wheeling, open, erotic, wild and 'feminine writing' would be welcomed by 'feminine' poets such as Arthur Rimbaud, Paul Éluard, Friedrich Hölderlin, Novalis and Rainer Maria Rilke, were they alive to read it. Compare Cixous' wildness (above) with Rimbaud's wildness (from, of course, *A Season in Hell*):

> C'est la vision des nombres. Nous allons à l'*Esprit*. C'est très certain, c'est oracle, ce que je dis. Je comprends, et ne sachant m'expliquer sans paroles païennes, je voudrais me taire. [...] Me voici sur la plage armoricaine. Que les villes s'allument dans le soir. Ma journée est faite; je quitte l'Europe. L'air marin brûlera mes poumons; les climats perdus me tanneront. Nager, broyer l'herbe, chasser, fumer surtout; boire des

> liqueurs fortes comme du métal bouillant, - comme faisaient ces chers ancêtres autour des feux.
> [It is the vision of numbers. We are moving towards *Spirit*. It is certain, this prophecy, I tell you. I understand and don't know how to explain it without using pagan words, I would rather keep quiet. [...] Here I am on the beach of Brittany. Let cities light up in the night. My day is done; I leave Europe. The sea air will burn my lungs; lost climates will tan me. To swim, to pound the grass, to hunt, to smoke above all, to drink strong liquors like bubbling metal, - like the dear ancestors did around the fires][5]

At times, Hélène Cixous moves into a poetic mode wholly in tune with Arthur Rimbaud, as in this passage from *Souffles* (*Breaths*, 1975):

> Her beauty strikes me. Produces streaming. Makes me flow. She seduces my forces. Gentleness. Gives me the desire to complete her. Emptying me. Destroys and commences me. *Da!* (C, 50)

Here Hélène Cixous employs the language of feminist erotica and makes it do the work of her own body-based feminism. For Cixous, as for Arthur Rimbaud, writing is a bliss of excess, in which writing becomes a flight, 'a flight of metaphors', to use Julia Kristeva's useful term. Cixous' writing is 'deeply metaphorical', straining to find the literal under the figurative, the living world, of flesh, under language (F. Defromont, 117).

> The language of love is impossible, inadequate, immediately allusive when one would like it to be most straightforward; it is a flight of metaphors - it is literature. (J. Kristeva, 1987, 1)

Hélène Cixous' writing, in her wild, idealistic mode, is constantly pushing at the limits of writing and language. It is always about to take poetic flight, to leap over the abyss, into the beyond, just like Arthur Rimbaud's poetry. 'Thunder of the gift. The voice there! Gives! Eagle! But first of all the tongue, violence of the adoration. I want. I listen. Flies!' (ib., 50) In *La venue à l'écriture*, Cixous writes:

> Let yourself go! Let go of everything! Lose everything! Take to the air. Take to the open sea. Take to letters. Listen: nothing is found. Nothing is lost. Everything remains to be sought. Go, fly, swim, bound, descend, cross, love the unknown, love the uncertain, love what has not yet been seen, love no one, whom you are, whom you will be, leave yourself, shrug off the old lies, *dare what you don't dare*, it is there that you will take pleasure never made your here anywhere but there, and rejoice, in the terror, follow it where you're afraid to go, go ahead, take the plunge, you're on the right trail! (40-41, V. Conley, 1992, 65)

This is Hélène Cixous writing at her most opened-out and excessive, yet this is a command that has often been shouted into the ether, this letting go and running free, this moving beyond and out, into the Open.[5] When Cixous continues, in *Coming to Writing*, to write in this way, it seems she is not 'writing *like*' Rimbaud, she *is* Rimbaud. It is a poetic ventriloquization of disarming persuasiveness:

> Gain your freedom: get rid of everything, vomit up everything, give up everything. Give up absolutely everything, do you hear me? *All of it!* (ib., 41)

HÉLÈNE CIXOUS, JULIA KRISTEVA AND ARTHUR RIMBAUD

Julia Kristeva has created a psychopoetry of the semiotic and the *chora*. These refer to archaic maternal spaces or modalities which help to create art and poetry. It is worth looking at Kristeva's notion of the semiotic modality and the *chora*, for it bears trenchantly on Hélène Cixous' poetics, and on Arthur Rimbaud's poetic quest, especially if one considers Rimbaud's deeply ambiguous œdipal feelings and his confused, anxious relationship with his mother.

Julia Kristeva breaks with Sigmund Freud and Jacques Lacan in her *chora* thesis: for she founds her philosophy of the *chora* not on the primacy of the phallus as 'transcendent signifier', as in the Lacanian system. Instead, there is a sublimation of maternal *jouissance*:

> At that point we witness the possibility of creation, of sublimation. I think that every type of creation, even if it's scientific, is due to this possibility of opening the norms, towards pleasure, which refers to an archaic experience with a maternal pre-object. ("A Question of Subjectivity", 131)

From the *chora* and semiotic, then, flows poetry. This is where things get very interesting. Artistic creation becomes a struggle involving signification, transgression, the semiotic and the symbolic.

> And so, according to psychoanalysis, poets as individuals fall under the category of fetishism [writes Kristeva]; the very practice of art necessitates reinvesting the maternal *chora* so that it transgresses the symbolic order... the poetic function therefore converges with fetishism; it is not, however, identical to it. What distinguishes the poetic function from the fetishist mechanism is that it maintains a *signification* (*Bedeutung*). All its paths into, indeed valorizations of, pre-symbolic semiotic stases not only require the ensured maintenance of this signification but also serve signification, even when they dislocate it. No text, no matter how 'musicalized', is devoid of meaning or signification; on the contrary, musicalization pluralizes meanings. We may say therefore that the text is not a fetish. (DL, 115-6)

The poetic zone Arthur Rimbaud and other poets speak of or strive for is similar to Julia Kristeva's notion of the dark, pre-œdipal space of the mother, the *chora*. Michael Payne defines Kristeva's *chora* thus: 'a nourishing and maternal, pre-verbal semiotic space or state in which the linguistic sign has not yet been articulated as the absence of an object' (239). Rimbaud's alchemy of the word is partly founded, like Kristeva's *chora*, on the maternal body as an actuality. As Kristeva writes in *Desire in Language*:

> Cells fuse, split, and proliferate; volumes grow, tissues stretch, and body fluids change rhythm, speeding up or slowing down. Within the body, growing as a graft, indomitable, there is an other. (237)

The 'other' is the child; the poet in Arthur Rimbaud is pregnant with a different sort of child: her/his art, the poem, the artwork as the Magical Child of alchemy. In *Revolution as Poetic Language*, Kristeva speaks of the *chora* as the place where 'the subject is both generated and negated' (28); it is 'a place of change, it is fluid, amorphous, 'pre-word', and, like a cell, divisible' (ib., 239-240n.). Language, though, can never circumscribe this maternal space: to name it is to change it.

In *Desire in Language* Julia Kristeva writes:

> Poetic language, the only language that uses up transcendence and theology to sustain itself; poetic language, knowingly the enemy of religion, by its very economy borders on psychosis (as for its subject) and totalitarianism or fascism (as for the institution it implies or evokes). (125)

This can apply to Arthur Rimbaud (Julia Kristeva thinks of Antonin Artaud, Vladimir Mayakovsky and Louis-Ferdinand Céline). Kristeva continues:

> Since at least Hölderlin, poetic language has deserted beauty and meaning to become a laboratory where, facing philosophy, knowledge, and the transcendental ego of all signification, the impossibility of a signified or signifying identity is being sustained. If we took this venture seriously – if we could hear the burst of black laughter it hurls at all attempts to master the human situation, to master language by language – we would be forced to re-examine "literary history', to rediscover beneath rhetoric and poetics its unchanging but always different polemic with the symbolic function. (*Desire in Language*, 145)

Julia Kristeva's description of the 'writer' is quite different from that imagined by newspaper columnists working for the middlebrow Sunday supplements, or visitors to the local public library (the sort of people that

Arthur Rimbaud despised):

> I shall term "writer" that ability to rebound whereby the violence of rejection, in extravagant rhythm, finds its way into a multiplied signifier. It is not the reconstruction of a unary subject, reminiscing, in hysterical fashion, about his lacks in meaning, his plunges into an underwater body. It is rather the return of the limit-as-break, castration, and the bar separating signifier from signified, which found naming, codification, and language; they do this not in order to vanish at that point (as communal meaning would have it), but in order, lucidly and consciously, to reject and multiply them, to dissolve even their boundaries, and to use them again. (DL, 187)

The poetic moment, for Julia Kristeva, is founded on desire: desire is what keeps the system together:

> The other that will guide you and itself through this dissolution is a rhythm, music, and within language, a text. But what is the connection that holds you both together? Counter-desire, the negative of desire, inside-out desire, capable of questioning (or provoking) its own infinite quest. Romantic, filial, adolescent, exclusive, blind and œdipal: it is all that, but for others. It returns to where you are, both of you, disappointed, irritated, ambitious, in love with history, critical, on the edge and even in the midst of its own identity crisis. (DL, 165)

Arthur Rimbaud's problem centred partly on the Muse, on the problem of inspiration and poetic energy.

> By the time Rimbaud proclaimed himself as the other [commented Jed Rasula], it was a gesture played out against the vacancy of what had formerly been confoundingly potent with Muses, however much his insurgence clamoured for a retrieval of the lost Muse.[3]

In "Baudelaire, or Infinity, Perfume, and Punk", Julia Kristeva speaks ironically of the outsider status of the artist in a bourgeois society which offers no refuge:

> If through a writing that is synonymous with the amatory condition –

> an experience at the limits of the identifiable – the writer can find no other place in the bosom of bourgeois society than that of a refugee at the side of nonproductive nobility or of the Church, which protects fetishes under the symbolic umbrella, we can only interpret that as an indictment of that very society rather than the evidence of the writer's error or "failure". (TL, 339)

Hélène Cixous demonstrates that writing is always taking place, even when the writer isn't writing. Writing is always occurring. Somewhere, writing is always happening. An on-going process, like life itself. Cixous is precious because she reminds us how valuable writing can be, how central it is to being alive. It's writing that goes beyond compulsion or obsession, it's writing as the foundation of life.

The last word should go to Hélène Cixous: she muses in *The Book of Promethea*:

> I think about the books I will never write, that I will never read perhaps, books that are nonetheless written, are being written in the depths, books I love, it is for them that I lean out so dangerously over the edge of the abyss. (97)

✣

ILLUSTRATIONS

Images of Hélène Cixous.

Images of some of the people who have influenced her, and people that she has studied.

On this page and the following pages
are some artists and thinkers discussed
by Hélène Cixous, and associated with her work.

Friedrich Nietzsche (below).

Arthur Rimbaud

Sigmund Freud

Jacques Derrida, above.
Jacques Lacan, below.

Monique Wittig

Luce Irigaray

Julia Kristeva

NOTES

PREFACE

1. S. Jackson: "Gender and Heterosexuality: A Materialist Feminist Analysis", in M. Maynard, 1994, 13.
2. S. Jackson, ib., 13; C. Delphy, 1995.
3. See Gayatri Chakravorty Spivak, 1981.

PART ONE: FRENCH FEMINISM

1 INTRODUCTORY

1. In the indexes of literary, feminist and cultural studies books, Hélène Cixous' name comes in between entries such as children, Christianity, Chodorow, cinema, Cinderella, Cicero, Circe, circumcision, civilization, civil rights, class, Claudel, Clément, clitoridectomy and clitoris. Citations of Hélène Cixous' writings in criticism include: L. Pietropaolo & A. Testaferri, eds. *Feminisms in the Cinema*, Indiana University Press, Bloomington, 1995; Pat Kirkham, ed. *The Gendered Object*,

Manchester University Press, 1996; Penny Florence & Dee Reynolds, eds. *Feminist subjects, multi-media: Cultural methodologies*, Manchester University Press, 1995; C. Hemmings, in J. Bristow & A. Wilson, eds. *Activating Theory, Gay, Bisexual Politics*, Lawrence & Wishart, 1993; J. Flynn in Barbara Gold *et al*, eds. *Sex and Gender in Medieval and Renaissance Texts: The Latin Tradition*, State University of New York Press, 1997; P. Cox: *Gender, Genre and the Romantic Poets*, Manchester University Press, 1996; R. Ballaster, in V. Sage & A. Smith, eds. *Modern Gothic: A Reader*, Manchester University Press, 1997.

2 FRENCH FEMINIST POETICS

FEMALE SEXUALITY

1. "A partir de Polylogue", interview with Françoise van Rossum-Guyon, *Revue des sciences humaines*, vol. XLIV, no. 168, tr. Seán Hand, Oct-Dec 1977, 495f.
2. Lynne Pykett. *Engendering Fictions*, Arnold, 1995, 12.
3. Gregory Woods: "The injured sex: Hemingway's voice of masculinist anxiety", in J. Still, 1993, 168.
4. H. Cixous: "Castration or Decapitation?", *Signs*, 7, 1, 52.
5. See Arleen B. Dallery; Deborah Cameron; Jan Montefiore; Andrea Nye: "The voice of the serpent: French feminism and the philosophy of language", in A. Garry, 1989.
6. Monique Wittig: "The Straight Mind", *Feminist Issues*, 1, 1, 110.
7. Luce Irigaray: *Parler n'est jamais neutre*, tr. David Macey, in I, 94.

FRIEDRICH NIETZSCHE AND FRENCH FEMINISM

1. See, for example, Kelly Oliver: "Who is Nietzsche's Woman?", in B. On, 1994; K. Oliver: "Nietzsche's 'Woman'", *Radical Philosophy*, 48, 1988; Jean Graybeal: *Language and "the Feminine" in Nietzsche and Heidegger*, Indiana University Press, Bloomington 1990; D. Krell, 1986; D. O'Hara, 1985; Sarah Kofman: *Nietzsche et la scéne philosophique*, Union générale d'éditions, Paris, 1979; S. Kofman: "Baubô", in M. Gillespie; Carol Diethe: "Nietzsche and the Woman Question", *History of European Ideas*, 11, 1989; Gary Schapiro: *Alcyone: Nietzsche on Gifts, Noise, and Women*, SUNY, Albany 1991; O. Schutte: "Nietzsche on Gender Difference", in B. On; Michael Platt: "Woman, Nietzsche, and Nature", *Maieutis*, 2, 1981; Gayle L. Ormiston: "Traces of Derrida: Nietzsche's Image of Woman", *Philosophy Today*, 28,

1984; L. Baker, 1989; E. Behler, 1988.

2. Jacques Derrida, *Spurs*, 101; see also D. Krell, 1986.
3. See Kelly Oliver, Sarah Kofman, op. cit.
4. Nietzsche: *Briefe an Peter Gast*, Leipzig, 1924, 89-90.
5. Janet Lungstrum: "Nietzsche Writing Woman/ Woman Writing Nietzsche", in P. Burgard, 144.
6. Sarah Kofman: *L'Enigma de la femme: La femme dans les textes de Freud*, Galilée, Paris, 1980. See also Biddy Martin: *Woman and Modernity: The (Life)Styles of Lou Andreas-Salomé*, Cornell University Press, Ithaca 1991.
7. L. Andreas-Salomé: "Die in sich ruhende Frau", in *Zur Psychologie der Frau*, ed. Giselda Brinker-Gabler, Fischer, Frankfurt, 1978, 295-6.
8. Both Arkady Plotinsky and Alan D. Schrift use Hélène Cixous' ecstatic text "The Laugh of the Medusa", and "Sorties" (A. Plotinsky and A. Schrift, both in P. Burgard).
9. See John Lechte: "Art, Love, and Melancholy in the Work of Julia Kristeva", in J. Fletcher, 39.
10. Kelly Oliver: "Nietzsche's Abjection", in P. Burgard, 60.
11. F. Nietzsche: *The Birth of Tragedy*, tr. W. Kaufmann, Vintage, New York, 1967, §16, 104.
12. F. Nietzsche: *Ecce Homo*, in *On the Genealogy of Morals and Ecce Homo*, Vintage, New York 1967, 266.
13. See P. Burgard, 235; see also S. Kofman, A. Schrift, J. Lungstrum, *et al*, in the same volume; also, Hélène Cixous' "Sorties" and *The Newly-Born Woman*.
14. F. Nietzsche: *The Gay Science*, tr. Walter Kaufmann, Vintage, New York, 1974, §72, 129.

JACQUES LACAN AND FRENCH FEMINISM

1. Luce Irigaray: *Speculum of the Other Woman* and *This Sex Which Is Not One*, both 1985; see also: Dorothy Leland: "Lacanian psychoanalysis and French feminism: toward an adequate political psychology", *Hypatia*, 3, 3, Winter, 1989, 81-103.
2. Elizabeth Grosz: "Refiguring Lesbian Desire", in L. Doan, 75.
3. R.M. Rilke, letter to Clara Rilke, 8 March, 1907, in *Gesammalte Briefe 1892-1926*, Insel Verlag, Leipzig, 1940, II, 279f.
4. Maggie Humm: "Is the gaze feminist? Pornography, film and feminism", *Perspectives on Pornography*, eds. G. Day & C. Bloom, Macmillan, 1988; L. Gamman, 1988; E.D. Pribram, 1988.
5. J. Lacan, "The meaning of the phallus", 1988; Bernard Baas: "Le désir pur", *Ornicar?*, 83, 1987; R. Lapsley, 1992.

6. C. Jung: *The Development of Personality*, vol. 17, Routledge, 1954, 198; Marie-Louise von Franz: *The Psychological Meaning of Redemption Motifs in Fairy Tales*, Inner City Books, Toronto, 1980, 39f.
7. Emma Jung & Marie-Louise von Franz: *The Grail Legend*, tr. Andrea Dykes, Sigo Press, Boston, Mass., 1980, 64.
8. Hélène Cixous writes: '[m]en say that there are two unrepresentable things: death and the feminine sex. That's because they need femininity to be associated with death; it's the jitters that give them a hard-on! For themselves! They need to be afraid of us' ("The Laugh of the Medusa", M, 255).
9. Larysa Mykyta: "Lacan, Literature and the Look", *SubStance* 39, 1983, 54.
10. See Laura Mulvey: "Visual pleasure and narrative cinema", *Screen*, 16, 3, 1975, 6-19.
11. Catherine King: "The Politics of Representation: A Democracy of the Gaze", in Frances Bonner *et al*, eds. *Imagining Women Cultural Representations and Gender*, Polity Press, Cambridge 1992, 136.
12. Luce Irigaray: "Women's Exile", in D. Cameron, 1990, 83; and Luce Irigaray: *Speculum*.
13. Emma Pérez: "Irigaray's Female Symbolic in the Making of Chicana Lesbian Sitios y Lenguas (Sites and Discourses)", in L. Doan, 108.

3 FRENCH FEMINISM, SEXUALITY, AND SEXUAL DIFFERENCE

SEXUAL DIFFERENCE

1. Xavière Gauthier, in M, 201-2.
2. L. Irigaray: "Ce sexe qui n'en est pas un", M, 103; see also: Jane Gallop, 1983, 77-83; Elizabeth Grosz: "Philosophy, subjectivity and the body", in C. Pateman & E. Grosz, 1986, 125-43.
3. Moira Gatens: "Power, Bodies and Difference", in M. Barrett, 1992, 134.
4. A. Jones: "Writing the Body", in E. Showalter, 1986, 369.
5. Chris Straayer: "The Hypothetical Lesbian Heroine in Narrative Feature Film", in C. Creekmur, 1995, 45
6. Audre Lorde: *Sister Outsider, Crossing Press,* New York, 1984, and in M. Humm 1992, 283.
7. Valerie Traub: "The Ambiguities of "Lesbian" Viewing Pleasure: The (Dis)articulations of *Black Widow*", in C. Creekmur, 1995, 135.
8. Cindy Patton: "Hegemony and Orgasm – or the Instability of Heterosexual Pornography", *Screen*, 30, 1/2, Spring, 1989, 100, 112.

9. Sue Miller: *The Good Mother*, Harper & Row, New York, 1986.
10. Summer Brenner: *The Soft Room,* Figures, 1978.
11. Susan Griffin: *Viyella*, in Laura Chester, 326.
12. See, for instance, Lonnie Barbach, ed. *Pleasures: Women Write Erotica,* Doubleday, New York, 1984; Laura Duesing: *Three West Coast Women*, Five Fingers Poetry, 1987; Clayton Eshleman, ed. *Caterpillar Anthology*, Anchor, 1971; Lynne Tillman: *Weird Fucks*, 1980; Jane Hirshfield: *Of Gravity and Angels,* Wesleyan University Press, 1988; Jayne Anne Phillips: *Black Tickets,* Delacorte Press, 1979; Marilyn Hacker: *Love, Death and the Changing of the Seasons,* Arbor House, 1986; Nancy Friday: *Forbidden Flowers: More Women's Sexual Fantasies*, Arrow, 1993.
13. Xavière Gauthier, in M, 201-2.
14. Liz Kotz: "Complicity: Women Artists Investigating Masculinities", in P. Gibson, 103.
15. Roland Barthes, in Mary Jacobus, 1979, 11.

LESBIAN, GAY AND QUEER THEORY

1. Heather Findlay: "Freud's "Fetishism" and the Lesbian Dildo Debates", in C. Creekmur, 1995, 329.
2. S. Freud: "Fetishism", *Standard Edition*, 21, 153f.
3. Elaine Marks, "Lesbian Intertextuality", in G. Stambolian, 376.
4. Marilyn Farewell: "Toward Definition of the Lesbian Literary Imagination", *Signs*, 14, 1988, 98.
5. Namascar Shaktini: "Displacing the Phallic Subject: Wittig's Lesbian Writing", *Signs*, 8, 1, Autumn, 1982, 29.

WOMEN AS WITCHES, OUTSIDERS, POETS

1. See M. Warner, 1985; Kenneth Clark: *The Nude*, Pantheon Books, 1957; Lynda Nead, 19.
2. Sherry B. Ortner: "Is Female to Male as Nature is to Culture", in M. Evans, ed. *The Woman Question*, Fontana, 1982.
3. Edwin Ardener: "Belief and the Problem of Women", in Shirley Ardener, ed. *Perceiving Women,* Halsted Press, New York, 1978.
4. Elaine Showalter: "Feminist Criticism in the Wilderness", in E. Showalter, 1986, 262-3; J. Roberts, 1991, 1-5.
5. Ann Rosalind Jones: "Writing the Body: L'Écriture Féminine", in E. Showalter, 1986, 363.
6. A. Jardine, "Opaque Texts", in N. Miller, 1986, 109.
7. Victor Burgin: "Geometry and Abjection", in J. Fletcher, 115-6.

8. Luce Irigaray: "La différence sexuelle", *Ethiope de la différence sexuelle*, Minuit, Paris, 1984, and in Toril Moi, 1988, 128.
9. J. Kristeva: "La femme, ce n'est jamais ça", *Tel Quel,* Autumn, 1974, in M, 135.
10. Richard Dyer: "Male Gay Porn: Coming to Terms", *Jump Cut,* 30, 1985.
11. Thomas Waugh: "Men's Pornography: Gay vs. Straight", in Creekmur, 1995, 319.
12. M. Duras, interview in *Signs*, Winter, 1975, in M, 175.
13. For Griselda Pollock, Julia Kristeva's emphasis in her æsthetics of painting on the 'feminine» encourages seeing 'woman as difference, inchoate, unspeakable, enigmatic, metaphor for all that is outside representation and meaning except as lack' ("Painting, Feminism, History", in M. Barrett, 1992, 157).
14. See Gayatri Spivak, in M. Krupnick, 177.
15. See Susan Rubin Suleiman: "(Re)Writing the Body: The Politics of Female Eroticism", in S. Suleiman, 14f; Elizabeth Grosz, 1988, 28-33; Alison M. Jagger, 1989; Naomi Schor, 1989, 38-58.
16. Monique Witting: "One Is Not Born a Woman", speech at the Feminist as Scholar Conference, May, 1979, Barnard College, New York.
17. E. Showalter: "Feminist Criticism in the Wilderness", in E. Showalter, 1986, 250.
18. French feminists, such as Hélène Cixous and Luce Irigaray, do not claim to 'represent' all women or 'women' as a concept (M. Gatens, in M. Barrett, 1992, 134).

PART TWO: HÉLÈNE CIXOUS

4 THE ECSTASY OF TEXTS

1. H. Cixous: "The Art of Innocence", C, 1994, 95.
2. For Gilles Deleuze, Hélène Cixous' texts are stroboscopic: they need to be read quickly once, then re-read slowly. ("Hélène Cixous ou l'écriture stroboscopique", *Le Monde*, 11 August, 1972, 10.)
3. 'It is precisely the assumption of a non-textual body outside of language, of a linguistic domain which is not itself corporeal that Cixous's reformation of mind-body relations in a feminine economy calls into question' (Barbara Freeman, 62).
4. M. Shiach, 1991, 16-23; V. Conley, 1992, 34; T. Moi, 1985, 102f; Alan D. Schrift, 210f; Arkady Plotinsky, 230f.
5. H. Cixous: "Who Are Free", 1993, 202-3.

6. "Le rire de la Méduse", 41, "The Laugh of the Medusa", M, 248.
7. H. Cixous: "Le dernier tableau ou le portrait de Dieu", *Entre l'écriture,* des femmes, Paris, 1986, 169-201.

5 HÉLÈNE CIXOUS, ARTHUR RIMBAUD AND THE FLIGHT OF POETS

1. H. Cixous, *Prénoms de personne [First Names of No One]*, 1974, C, 29.
2. See L.S. Salzberger. *Hölderlin,* Cambridge University Press, Cambridge, 1952, 8-12.
3. Ronald Peacock. *Hölderlin,* Methuen, 1973, 156.
4. A. Rimbaud, 'Bad Blood', *Complete Works*, 176.
5. 'All the characteristics of Cixous' practice point to freedom... Her tongues of ecstasy are then set free and they flow, spill, and stream in every direction, producing the very ebullience of ecstatic creation.' (Françoise Defromont, 123.)

HÉLÈNE CIXOUS, JULIA KRISTEVA AND ARTHUR RIMBAUD

1. J. Kristeva, *About Chinese Women*, in M. Eagleton, ed., 1991, 81.
2. Luce Irigaray: *Ce sexe qui n'en est pas un,* Minuit, Paris, 1977, in E. Marks, 103.
3. Jed Rasula: "Gendering the Muse", *Sulfur,* no. 35, Fall, 1994, 173.

BIBLIOGRAPHY

Titles in English are published in London, England, unless otherwise stated.
Titles in French are published in Paris, France, unless otherwise stated.

HÉLÈNE CIXOUS

The Exile of James Joyce, Calder, 1976

Angst, tr. Jo Levy, Calder, 1985

The Newly Born Woman, tr. Betsy Wing, Minnesota University Press, Minneapolis, 1986

Inside, tr. Carol Barko, Schocken Books, New York, 1986

Tancredi Continues, tr. Ann Liddle & Susan Sellers, in S. Sellers, 1988

Reading With Clarice Lispector, tr. Verena Andermatt Conley, Minnesota University Press, Minneapolis, 1990

The Book of Promethea, tr. Betsy Wing, University of Nebraska Press, Lincoln, 1991

"Coming to Writing" and Other Essays, tr. Sarah Cornell *et al,* Harvard University Press, Cambridge, 1991
Three Steps on the Ladder of Writing, tr. Sarah Cornell & Susan Sellers, Columbia University Press, New York, 1993
The Hélène Cixous Reader, ed. Susan Sellers, Routledge, 1994
Manna to the Mandelstams to the Mandelas, tr. Catherine MacGillivray, University of Minnesota Press, Minneapolis, 1995
Readings: The Poetics of Blanchot, Joyce, Kleist, Kafka, Lispector and Tsvetayeva, ed. Verena Andermatt Conley, University of Minnesota Press, Minneapolis, 1995

Dedans, Grasset, 1969
Le Troisème Corps, Grasset, 1970
Les Commencements, Grasset, 1970
Neutre, Grasset, 1972
Tombe, Seuil, 1973
Portrait du soleil, Denoël, 1974
Prénoms de personne, Seuil, 1974
Révolutions pour d'un Faust, Seuil, 1975
Souffles, des femmes, 1975
Là, Gallimard, 1976
Portrait de Dora, des femmes, 1976
Partie, des femmes, 1976
Angst, des femmes, 1977
Vivre le orange, des femmes, 1979
Anankè, des femmes, 1979
Illa, des femmes, 1980
(With) Ou l'art de l'innocence, des femmes, 1981
Limonade tout était si infini, des femmes, 1982
Entre l'écriture, des femmes, 1986
Manne, des femmes, 1988
L'heure de Clarice Lispector, des femmes, 1989
Jours de l'an, des femmes, 1990
L'ange secret, des femmes, 1991
Déluge, des femmes, 1992
Beethoven à jamais, ou l'éxistence de Dieu, Des femmes, 1993
La Fiancée juive, Des femmes, 1997
OR. Les lettres de mon père, Des femmes, 1997
Voiles (with Jacques Derrida), Galilée, 1998
Osnabrück, Des femmes, 1999
Les Rêveries de la femme sauvage. Scènes primitives, Galilée, 2000
Le Jour où je n'étais pas là, Galilée, 2000

Benjamin à Montaigne. Il ne faut pas le dire, Galilée, 2001
Manhattan. Lettres de la préhistoire, Galilée, 2002
Rêve je te dis, Galilée, 2003
L'Amour du loup et autres remords, Galilée, 2003
Tours promises, Galilée, 2004
L'amour même dans la boîte aux lettres, Galilée, 2005
Hyperrêve, Galilée, 2006

"Joyce: la (r)use de écriture", *Poétique*, 4, 1970
"The Character of Character", *New Literary History*, 5, 2, 1974
"Le rire de la Méduse", *L'Arc*, 61, 1975
"Fiction and Its Phantoms: A Reading of Freud's Das Unheimliche", *New Literary History*, 7, 3, 1976
"La Missexualité, où jouis-je?", *Poétique*, 26, 1976
"Le Sexe ou la tête?", *Les Cahiers du GRIF*, 13, 1976, tr. as "Castration or decapitation?", 1981
"Castration or Decapitation?", tr. A. Kuhn, *Signs*, 7, 1, 1981
"Le dernier tableau ou le portrait de Dieu", *Entre l'écriture*, des femmes, Paris, 1986
"The two countries of writing", in J. MacCannell, 1990
"Who Are Free, Are We Free?", *Critical Inquiry*, 12, 2, Winter, 1993
"Difficult Joys", in H. Wilcox, 1990

interview with Christiane Makward, *SubStance*, 5, Autumn, 1976
interview with Françoise van Rossum-Guyon, "Entretien avec Hélène Cixous", *Revue des sciences huines*, 168, 1977
& Madeleine Gagnon, Annie Leclerc: *La venue à l'écriture*, Union générale d'éditions 1977
interview with Verena Andermatt Conley, "An Exchange with Hélène Cixous" and "A Later Interview with Hélène Cixous"", in V. Conley, 1991, 129-178

OTHERS

L. Alcoff. "Cultural Feminism Versus Post-structuralism", *Signs*, 13, 3, 1988

C. Allen & J. Howard, eds. *Provoking Feminisms,* Chicago University Press, 2000

Keith Ansell-Pearson & Howard Caygill, eds. *The Fate of the New Nietzsche*, Avebury 1993

I. Armstrong, ed. *New Feminist Discourse*, Routledge, 1992

Alison Assister. *Althusser and Feminism,* Pluto Press, 1990

—. & Avedon Carol, eds. *Bad Girls and Dirty Pictures: The Challenge to Reclaim Feminism,* Pluto Press, 1993

Margaret Attack "The Other Feminist", *Paragraph*, 8, 1986

—. & Phil Powrie, eds. *Contemporary French Fiction by Women*, Manchester University Press, 1990

D. Attridge & M. Ferrer, eds. *Post-Stucturalist Joyce,* Cambridge University Press, Cambridge, 1984

Lang Baker. "Irigaray contre Bataille: Locating the Feminine in Nietzsche", *Social Discourse,* 2, 1989

Francis Barker *et al*, eds. *The Politics of Theory: The Proceedings of the Essex Conference on the Psychology of Literature,* University of Essex, Colchester, 1983

S. Barker, ed. *Signs of Change: Premodern, Modern, Postmodern*, State University of New York Press, 1996

Michèle Barrett & Anne Phillips, eds. *Destablizing Theory: Contemporary Feminist Debates*, Polity Press, 1992

Roland Barthes: *The Pleasure of the Text*, Hill and Wang, New York, 1975

—*Mythologies*, Hill & Wang, New York, 1972

—*S/Z*, Hill and Wang, New York, 1974

—*Image, Music, Text*, tr. Stephen Heath, Fontana, 1984

Elaine Hoffman Baruch & Lucienne Serrano. *Women Analyse Women in France, England and the United States,* Harvester Wheatsheaf, 1988

Gwendolyn Bays. *The Orphic Vision: Seer Poets from Novalis to Rimbaud,* University of Nebraska Press, Lincoln, 1964

Ruth Behar, ed. *Women Writing Culture,* University of California Press, Berkeley, 1995

Ernst Behler. *Derrida-Nietzsche/ Nietzsche-Derrida,* Schöningh, Munich, 1988

D. Bell & B. Kennedy, eds. *The Cybercultures Reader*, Routledge, 2000

R. Bell & R. Klein, eds. *Radically Speaking: Feminism Reclaimed,* Spinifex, North Melbourne, 1996

Catherine Belsey. *Critical Practice,* Routledge, 1980
—. *Desire: Love Stories in Western Culture,* Blackwell, 1994
Mary Berg: "Escaping the Cave: Luce Irigaray and Her Feminist Critics", in Gary Wihl & David Williams, eds. *Literature and Ethics,* McGill, Kingston, 1988
L. Berlant. "Live Sex Acts", *Feminist Studies,* 21, 2, 1995
J. Birringer. *Theatre, Theory, Postmodernism,* Indiana University Press, Bloomington, 1991
Harold Bloom, ed. *Arthur Rimbaud,* Chelsea House Publishers, New York, 1988
G. Bock & S. James, ed. *Beyond Equality and Difference,* Routledge, 1992
R. Braidotti. "On the Feminist Female Subject or, From the She-self to the She-other", in Bock, 1992
E. Brater, ed. *Feminine Focus: The New Women Playwrights,* Oxford University Press, Oxford, 1989
Teresa Brennan, ed. *Between Feminism and Psychoanalysis,* Routledge, 1989
A. Briggs & P. Cobley, eds. *The Media,* Longman, 1998
S. Bright, ed. *Herotica: A Collection of Women's Erotic Fiction,* Down There Press, San Francisco, 1988
—. & J. Blank, eds. *Herotica 2,* Plume, N.Y., 1992
—. ed. *Herotica 3,* Plume, N.Y., 1994
Peter Brooker, ed. *Modernism/ Postmodernism,* Longman, 1992
—. & P. Widdowson, eds. *A Practical Reader in Contemporary Literary Theory,* Prentice-Hall, 1996
A. Brooks. *Postfeminisms: Feminism, Cultural Theory and Cultural Forms,* Routledge, 1997
L. Brouwer *et al,* eds. *Beyond Limits,* University of Groningen Press, Groningen, 1990
B. Brown & P. Adams. "The feminine body and feminist politics", *M/F,* 3, 1979
Wendy Brown. "Hesitations, Postmodern Exposures", *differences,* 3, 1, 1991
David Buckingham, ed. *Reading Audiences,* Manchester University Press, 1995
Peter J. Burgard, ed. *Nietzsche and the Feminine,* University Press, of Virginia, Charlottesville, 1994
Victor Burgin *et al,* eds. *Formations of Fantasy,* Methuen, 1986
Carolyn Burke. "Rethinking the maternal", in H. Eisenstein, 1980
Judith Butler. *Gender Trouble: Feminism and the Subversion of Identity,* Routledge, 1990
—. & J.W. Scott, eds. *Feminists Theorise the Political,* Routledge, 1992

—. *Bodies That Matter*, Routledge, 1993
—. *Subjects of Desire: Hegelian Reflections in 20th Century France*, Columbia University Press, 1999
—. *Antigone's Claim: Kinship Between Life and Death*, Judith Butler, Columbia University Press, 2002
Colette Camelin. "La Scène de la fille dans *Illa*", *Littérature*, 67, Oct, 1987
Beatrice Cameron. "Letter to Hélène Cixous", *SubStance*, 17, 1977
Deborah Cameron, ed. *The Feminist Critique of Language: A Reader*, Routledge, 1990
Claudia Card, ed. *Adventures in Lesbian Philosophy*, Indiana University Press, 1994
S.-E. Case, ed. *Performing Feminisms: Feminist Critical Theory and Theatre*, Johns Hopkins University Press, Baltimore, 1990
John Caughie & Annette Kuhn, eds. *The Sexual Subject: A* Screen *Reader in Sexuality*, Routledge, 1992
K. Champagne. ""Stop Reading Films": Film Studies, Close Analysis and Gay Pornography", *Cinema Journal*, 36, 4, 1997
L. Cherny & E.R. Weise, eds. *Wired Women: Gender and New Realities in Cyberspace*, Seal Press, Seattle, 1996
Gail Chester & Julienne Dickey, ed. *Feminism and Censorship: The Current Debate*, Prism Press, Bridport, Dorset, 1988
Laura Chester, ed. *Deep Down: New Sensual Writing By Women*, Faber, 1987
Richard A. Cohen, ed. *Face to Face with Levinas*, State University Press, of New York, Albany, 1986
Alex Comfort. *I and That*, Beazley, 1979
Verena Andermatt Conley. "Hélène Cixous and the Uncovery of Feminine Language", *Women and Literature*, 7, 1, 1977
—. *Hélène Cixous: Writing the Feminine*, University of Nebraska Press, Lincoln 1984
—. ed. *Boundary* 2, 12, Winter, 1984, Cixous number
—. *Hélène Cixous: Writing the Feminine*, University of Nebraska Press, Lincoln 1991
—. *Hélène Cixous*, Harvester Wheatsheaf, 1992
Joseph Cornell. *Theatre of the Mind: Selected Diaries, Letters, and Files*, ed. Mary Ann Caws, Thames & Hudson, 1993
C.K. Creekmur & A. Doty, eds. *Out in Culture: Gay, Lesbian, and Queer Essays on Popular Culture*, Cassell, 1995
Diane Griffin Crowder. "Amazons and mothers? Monique Wittig, Hélène Cixous and theories of women's writing", *Contemporary Literature*, 24, Summer, 1983
Arleen Dallery. "The Politics of Writing (the) Body: Écriture Féminine", in

A. Jaggar, 1989
Mary Daly. *Pure Lust: Elemental Feminist Philosophy,* Women's Press, 1984
G. Day & C. Bloch, eds. *Perspectives on Pornography: Sexuality in Film and Literature,* Macmillan, 1988
Simone de Beauvoir. *The Second Sex*, Penguin, 1972
E. De Grazia. *Girls Lean Back Everywhere: The Law of Obscenity and the Assault On Genius*, Random House, N.Y., 1992
R. Delgado & J. Stefancic. *Must We Defend Nazis? Hate Speech, Pornography, and the New First Amendment,* New York University Press, 1997
J. De Mul. *Romantic Desire in (Post)Modern Art and Philosophy,* State University of New York Press, 1999
Jacques Derrida: *Writing and Difference,* University of Chicago Press, 1987
—*Of Grammatology*, John Hopkins University Press, Baltimore, 1976
—*'Speech and Phenomena' and Other Essays on Husserl's Theory of Signs*, tr. David B. Allison, Northwestern University Press, Evanston, 1973
—*Spurs: Nietzsche's Styles*, University of Chicago Press, Chicago, 1979
P. Deutscher & K. Oliver, eds. *Enigmas: Essays on Sarak Kofman,* Cornell University Press, Ithaca, 1999
Laura Doan, ed. *The Lesbian Postmodern*, Columbia University Press, New York, 1994
Mary Ann Doane. *The Desire to Desire: The Woman's Film of the 1940's,* Macmillan, 1988
B. Dow. *Prime Time Feminism: Television, Media Culture and the Women's Movement Since 1970,* University of Pennsylvania Press, Philadelphia, 1996
A. Dow. *Window Shopping: Cinema and the Postmodern,* University of California Press, Berkeley, 1993
Claire Duchen. *Feminism in France From May '68 to Mitterand,* Routledge, 1986
—. ed. *French Connections: Voices From the Women's Movement in France,* Hutchinson, 1987
Rachel DuPlessis. "For the Etruscans", in E. Showalter, 1986
J. Duran. *Toward a Feminist Epistemology*, Savage, Rowman & Littlefield, 1991
Brian Duren. "Cixous' Exorbitant Texts", *SubStance*, 10, 1981
Andrea Dworkin. *Pornography: Men Possessing Women,* Women's Press, 1984
—. *Intercourse*, Arrow, 1988
—. *Letters From a War Zone,* Secker & Warburg, 1988
—. *Mercy*, Arrow, 1990

Mary Eagleton, ed. *Feminist Literary Theory: A Reader*, Blackwell, 1986
—. ed. *Feminist Literary Criticism*, Longman, 1991
Anthony Easthope, ed. *Contemporary Film Theory*, Longman, 1993
H. Eilberg-Schwartz & W. Doniger, eds. *Off With Her Head! The Denial of Women's Identity in Myth, Religion, and Culture*, University Press, Berkeley, 1995
Hester Eisenstein & Alice Jardine, eds. *The Future of Difference*, Barnard College Women's Center, New York, 1980
—. *Contemporary Feminist Thought*, Unwin Paperbacks, 1984
K. Ellis, *et al*, eds. *Caught Looking: Feminism, Pornography and Censorship*, Caught Looking, N.Y., 1986
M. Ellman, ed. *Thinking about Women*, Virago, 1979
J. Epstein & K. Straub, eds. *Body Guards: The Cultural Politics of Gender Ambiguity*, Routledge, New York, 1991
S. Faludi. *Backlash*, Chatto, 1992
M. Farwell. *Heterosexual Plots and Lesbian Narratives*, New York University Press, 1996
Christine Faure. "The twilight of the goddesses, or the intellectual crisis of French feminism", *Signs*, 7, 1981
R. Felski. *Beyond Feminist Aesthetics: Feminist Literature and Social Change*, Hutchinson, 1989
Josette Féral. "Antigone or the irony of the tribe", *Diacritics*, Autumn, 1978
—. "The Powers of Difference", in H. Eisenstein, 1980
Claudine Fisher. *La Cosmogonie d'Hélène Cixous*, Rodopi, Amsterdam, 1988
J. Flax: "Postmodernism and Gender Relations in Feminist Theory", *Signs*, 12, 4, 1987;
John Fletcher & Andrew Benjamin, ed. *Abjection, Melancholia and Love: The Work of Julia Kristeva*, Routledge, 1990
Barbara Freeman. "Plus corps donc plus écriture: Hélène Cixous and the Mind-Body Problem", *Paragraph*, 11, 1, 1988
Sigmund Freud. *Standard Edition of the Complete Psychological Works of Sigmund Freud*, 24 vols, ed. James Strachey, Hogarth Press, 1953-74
Françoise Defromont: "Metaphorical Thinking and Poetic Writing in Virginia Woolf and Hélène Cixous", in H. Wilcox, 1990
Diana Fuss. *Essentially Speaking*, Routledge, New York, 1989
—. ed. *Inside/ Out: Lesbian Theories, Gay Theories*, Routledge, 1991
Jane Gallop. *Feminism and Psychoanalysis: The Daughter's Seduction*, Macmillan, 1982
—. *Thinking Through the Body*, Columbia University Press, New York, 1988
S. Gamble, ed. *The Icon Critical Dictionary of Feminism and Postfeminism*,

Icon, Cambridge, 1999
Lorraine Gamman & Margaret Marshment, eds. *The Female Gaze: Women as Viewers of Popular Culture,* Women's Press, 1988
—. & M. Makinen. *Female Fetishism,* Lawrence & Wishart, 1994
Ann Garry & Marilyn Pearsal, eds. *Women, Knowledge and Reality: explorations in feminist philosophy,* Unwin Hyman 1989
Xavière Gauthier: "Pourquoi Sorcières?", in *Sorcières,* 1, 1976, in E. Marks, 1981
Elissa D. Gelfand & Virginia Thorndike Hules. *French Feminist Criticism,* Garland, New York, 1985
Anna Gibbs. "Cixous and Gertrude Stein", *Meanjin,* 38, 1979
Pamela Church Gibson & Roma Gibson, ed. *Dirty Looks: Women, Pornography, Power,* British Film Institute, 1993
André Gide. *Logbook of The Coiners,* tr. Justin O'Brien, Cassell, 1952
—. *Journals 1889-1949,* ed. & tr. Justin O'Brien, Penguin, 1967
—. *The Counterfeiters,* tr. Dorothy Bussy, Penguin, 1966
Sandra Gilbert. "A tarantella of history", introduction to Cixous, *The Newly Born Woman*
M.A. Gillespie & T.B. Strong, eds. *Nietzsche: Explorations in Philosophy, Aesthetics, and Politics,* University of Chicago Press, Chicago, 1988
J. Gordon & V. Hollinger, eds. *Blood Read: The Vampire As Metaphor in Contemporary Culture,* University of Pennsylvania Press, Philadelphia, 1997
Robert Graves. *The White Goddess,* Faber, 1961
Gayle Greene & Coppélia Kahn, eds. *Making a Difference: Feminist Literary Criticism,* Methuen, 1985
Gabriele Griffin, *Outwrite: Lesbianism and Popular Culture,* Pluto Press, 1993
—. *et al,* eds. *Stirring It: Challenges For Feminism,* Taylor & Francis, 1994
Susan Griffin. *Pornography and Silence: Culture's Revenge Against Nature,* Women's Press, 1981
Morwenna Griffiths & Margaret Whitford, eds. *Feminist Perspectives in Philosophy,* Indiana University Press, Bloomington, 1988
E. Grosz. "Philosophy, Subjectivity and the Body", in C. Pateman, 1986
—. "Corporeal Feminism", *Australian Feminist Studies,* 5, Summer, 1987
—. "Desire, the body and recent French feminism", *Intervention,* 21-2, 1988
—. *Sexual Subversions,* Allen & Unwin, 1989
—. "The Body of Signification", in J. Fletcher, 1990
—. *Jacques Lacan: A Feminiist Introduction,* Routeldge, 1990
—. "Lesbian fetishism?", *Differences,* 3, 2, 1991
—. "Fetishization", in E. Wright, 1992

—. "Julia Kristeva", in E. Wright, 1992
—. *Volatile Bodies*, Indiana University Press, Bloomington, 1994
—. "Refiguring Lesbian Desire", in Doan, 1994
—. *Space, Time and Perversion*, Routledge, 1995
S. Gubar. *Critical Condition: Feminism and the Turn of the Century*, Columbia University Press, 2000
Susan J. Hekman. *Gender and Knowledge: Elements of a Postmodern Feminism*, Polity Press, 1990
Phillip Herring. "Joyce and Rimbaud", in S.B. Busrui & B. Benstock, eds. *James Joyce: An International Perspective*, Barnes & Noble, Totowa, New Jersey, 1982
Molly Hite. "Writing - and reading - the body: female sexuality and recent feminist fiction", *Feminist Studies*, 14, 1, 1988
K. Hohne & H. Wussow, eds. *A Dialogue of Voices: Feminist Literary Theory and Bakhtin*, University of Minnesota Press, Minneapolis, 1994
Friedrich Hölderlin. *Poems and Fragments*, tr. Michael Hamburger, Anvil Press, 1994
Christine Holmlund. "I Love Luce: The Lesbian, Mimesis and Masquerade in Irigaray, Freud, and Mainstream Film", *New Formations*, 8, Autumn, 1989
Maggie Humm. *Feminisms: A Reader*, Harvester Wheatsheaf, 1992
—. ed. *The Dictionary of Feminist Theory*, Harvester Wheatsheaf, 1995
I. Hunter *et al. On Pornography*, St Martin's Press, N.Y., 1993
Andreas Huyssen. *After the Great Divide: Modernism, Mass Culture, Postmodernism*, Indiana University Press, Bloomington, 1986
Luce Irigaray. *This Sex Which Is Not One*, tr. C. Porter & C. Burke, Cornell University Press, New York, 1977
—*Speculum of the Other Woman*, tr. G.C. Gill, Cornell University Press, New York, 1985
—. *The Irigaray Reader*, ed. Margaret Whitford, Blackwell, Oxford, 1991
—*Marine Lover of Friedrich Nietzsche*, tr. G.C. Gill, Columbia University Press, New York, 1991
—*Je, tu, nous: Toward a Culture of Difference*, tr. Alison Martin, Routledge, 1993
—*Thinking the Difference: For a Peaceful Revolution*, Athlone Press, 1994
—*An Ethics of Sexual Difference*, Athlone, 1993
S. Jackson & J. Jones, eds. *Contemporary Feminist Theories*, Edinburgh University Press, 1998
Mary Jacobus, ed. *Women Writing and Writing About Women*, Croom Helm, 1979
—. "Is There a Woman In This Text?", *New Literary History*, 14, 1982
—. *Reading Woman: essays in feminist criticism*, Methuen, 1986

—. "Madonna: Like a Virgin, or, Freud, Kristeva, and the Case of the Missing Mother", *Oxford Literary Review*, 8, 1986

—. ed. *Body/ Politics*, Routledge, 1990

A. Jaggar & S.R. Bordo, eds. *Gender/ Body/ Knowledge: Feminist Reconstructions of Being and Knowing*, Rutgers University Press, New Brunswick, 1989

Alice Jardine. *Gynesis*, Cornell University Press, New York, 1985

—. "Opaque Texts", in N. Miller, 1986

—. & Anne M. Menke. "Exploding the Issue: 'French' 'Women' 'Writers' and 'the Canon'?", *Yale French Studies*, 75, 1988

—. & Anne Menke, eds. *Shifting Scenes: interviews on women, writing and politics in post '68 France*, Columbia University Press, New York, 1991

Karla Jay, ed. *Lesbian Erotics*, New York University Press, 1995

Ann Rosalind Jones. "Writing the Body: Toward an Understanding of L'Écriture féminine", in E. Showalter, 1986

Jordan Jones. "Renewing the Dance: René Daumal, the Surrealism of the Bardo, and Shamanic Poetry", *Heaven Bone*, 11, Spring, 1994

N.W. Jouve: "Hélène Cixous", in H. Wilcox, 1990

—. *White Woman Speaks With Forked Tongue*, Routledge, 1991

—. *Our Voices, Ourselves*, Peter Lang, New York, 1991

C. Juncker. "Writing (with) Cixous", *College English*, 50, 4, 1988

C.G. Jung. *Memories, Dreams, Reflections*, Collins, 1967

W. Kendrick. *The Secret Museum: Pornography in Modern Culture*, Viking, 1987

Kensington Ladies' Erotica Society. *Ladies' Own Erotica*, Ten Speed Press, Berkeley, 1984

A. Kibbey *et al. Sexual Artifice: Persons, Images, Politics*, New York University Press, 1994

Laura Kipnis. "Feminism: The Political Conscience of Postmodernism?", in P. Brooker, 1992

A. Koedt *et al*, eds. *Radical Feminism*, Quadrangle Books. N.Y., 1970

S. Kofman. *Camera Obscura of Ideology*, Cornell University Press, 1999

Vivian Kogan. "I Want Vulva? Hélène Cixous and the Poetics of the Body", *L'Esprit créateur*, 25, 2, Summer, 1985

David Farrell Krell. *Postponement: Women, Sensuality, and Death in Nietzsche*, Indiana University Press, Bloomington, 1986

—. & David Woods. *Exceedingly Nietzsche: Aspects of Contemporary Nietzsche-Interpretation*, Routledge, 1988

Julia Kristeva. *About Chinese Women*, tr. A. Barrows, Boyars, 1977

—. *Polylogue*, Seuil, 1977

—. *Desire in Language: A Semiotic Approach to Literature and Art*, ed. L.S. Roudiez, tr. Thomas Gora *et al*, Blackwell 1982

—. *Powers of Horror: An Essay on Abjection,* tr. L.S. Roudiez, Columbia University Press, New York, 1982

—. *Revolution in Poetic Language,* tr. Margaret Walker, Columbia University Press, New York, 1984

—. *The Kristeva Reader,* ed. Toril Moi, Blackwell 1986

—. *Tales of Love,* tr. L.S. Roudiez, Columbia University Press, New York, 1987

—. *Black Sun: Depression and Melancholy,* tr. L.S. Roudiez, Columbia University Press, New York, 1989

—. *Language, The Unknown: An Initiation into Linguistics,* tr. Anne M. Menke, Harvester Wheatsheaf 1989

—. *Strangers to Ourselves,* tr. L.S. Roudiez, Harvester Wheatsheaf 1991

—. "A Question of Subjectivity: an interview" [with Susan Sellers], *Women's Review,* 12, 1986, in P. Rice, 1992

Annette Kuhn. "Introduction to Hélène Cixous's Castration or Decapitation?", *Signs,* 7, 1, 1981

—. *Women's Pictures: Feminism and the cinema,* Routledge & Kegan Paul, 1982

Jacques Lacan and the École Freudienne. *Écrits: A Selection,* tr. Alan Sheridan, Tavistock, 1977

—. *Feminine Sexuality,* eds. Juliet Mitchell and Jacqueline Rose, Macmillan, 1988

D. Landry & G. MacLean. *Unbearable Weight,* Blackwell, Oxford, 1993

Rob Lapsley & Michael Westlake. "From *Casablanca* to *Pretty Woman*: The Politics of Romance", *Screen,* 33, 1, Spring, 1992

Teresa de Laurentis, ed. *Feminist Studies/ Critical Studies,* Macmillan, 1988

John Lechte: *Julia Kristeva,* Routledge 1990 (a)

—"Art, Love, and Melancholy in the Work of Julia Kristeva", in J. Fletcher, 1990 (b)

S. Lefanu. *In the Chinks of the World Machine: Feminism and Science Fiction,* Women's Press, 1988

Lesbian History Group, eds. *Not a Passing Phase: Reclaiming Lesbians in History, 1840-1985,* Women's Press, 1989

Philip Lewis. "Revolutionary Semiotics", *Diacritics,* 4, 3, Autumn, 1974

Cecile Lindsay. "Body Language: French Feminist Utopias", *The French Review,* 60, 1, Oct, 1986

T. Lorraine. *Irigaray and Deleuze,* Cornell University Press, 1999

JoAnn Loulan. *The Lesbian Erotic Dance: Butch, Femme, Androgyny, and Other,* Spinsters, San Francisco, 1990

T. Lowry. *The Classic Clitoris: Historic Contributions to Scientific Sexuality,* Belson, Chicago, 1978

N. Lykke & R. Braidotti, eds. *Between Monsters, Goddesses and Cyborgs*, Zed Books, 1996
Juliet Flower MacCannell, ed. *The Other Perspective in Gender and Culture: Rewriting Women and the Symbolic*, Columbia University Press, New York, 1990
Christiane Makward. "Interview with Hélène Cixous", *SubStance*, 5, 1976
Elaine Marks & Isabelle de Courtivron, eds. *New French Feminisms: an Anthology*, Harvester Wheatsheaf, 1981
M. Maynard & J. Purvis, eds. *Researching Woman's Lives*, Taylor & Francis, 1994
R. McRuer. *The Queer Renaissance*, New York University Press, 1997
Geraldine Meaney. *(Un)Like Subjects: Women, Theory, Fiction*, Routledge, 1993
R. Michael *et al*. *Sex in America: A Definitive Survey*, Little, Brown, 1994
Elaine Millard. "French Feminisms", in S. Mills, 1996
N.K. Miller, ed. *The Poetics of Gender*, Columbia University Press, New York, 1986
R. Miller. *Bunny: The Real Story fo Playboy*, Rinehart & Winston, N.Y., 1984
Kate Millett. *Sexual Politics*, Doubleday, Garden City, 1970
Sara Mills, ed. *Gendering the Reader*, Harvester Wheatsheaf, 1993
—. *et al*, eds. *Feminist Readings/ Feminists Reading*, University Press, of Virginia, Charlottesville, 1996
T. Modleski, ed. *Studies in Entertainment*, Indiana University Press, Bloomington, 1987
—. *The Women Who Knew Too Much: Hitchcock and Feminist Theory*, Methuen, 1988
—. *Feminism Without Women: Culture and Criticism in a 'Postfeminist' Age*, Routledge, 1991
Toril Moi. *Sexual/ Textual Politics: Feminist Literary Theory*, Routledge, 1988
—. ed. *French Feminist Thought*, Blackwell, 1988
Jan Montefiore. *Feminism and Poetry: Language, Experience, Identity in Women's Writing*, Pandora, 1987
Moira Monteith, ed. *Women's Writing: A Challenge to Theory*, Harvester Press, Brighton, Sussex, 1986
Pam Morris *Literature & Feminism*, Blackwell, 1993
Raoul Mortley. *French Philosophers in Conversation: Derrida, Irigaray, Levinas, Le Doeuff, Schneider, Serres*, Routledge, 1991
Martine Motard-Noard. *Les Fictions d'Hélène Cixous*, French Forum Publishers, Lexington, 1992
Laura Mulvey. *Visual and Other Pleasures*, Macmillan, 1989
Sally Munt, ed. *New Lesbian Criticism: Literary and Cultural Readings*,

Harvester Wheatsheaf, 1992
J. Nagle, ed. *Whores and Other Feminists*, Routledge, N.Y., 1997
Lynda Nead. *Female Nude: Art, Obscenity and Sexuality*, Routledge, 1992
M. Negron, ed. *Lectures de la différence sexuelle*, de femmes Antoinette Fouquet, Paris, 1994
Joan Nestle, ed. *The Persistent Desire: A Femme-Butch Reader*, Alyson, Boston, 1992
L. Nicholson, ed. *Feminism/ Postmodernism*, Routledge, 1990
Friedrich Nietzsche. *A Nietzsche Reader*, ed. R.J. Hollingdale, Penguin, 1977
Andrea Nye. "Preparing the way for a feminist praxis", *Hypatia*, 1, 1986
D.T. O'Hara, ed. *Why Nietzsche Now?*, Indiana University Press, Bloomington, 1985
D. Olkowski, ed. *Resistance, Flight, Creation: Feminist Enactments of French Philosophy*, Cornell University Press, 2000
Bat-Ami Bar On, ed. *Modern Engendering: Critical Feminist Readings in Modern Western Philosophy*, State University of New York Press, Albany 1994
Camille Paglia. *Sex, Art and American Culture*, Viking, 1992
—. *Vamps and Tramps: New Essays*, Penguin, 1995
Carole Pateman & Elizabeth Grosz, eds. *Feminist Challenges*, Allen & Unwin, Sydney, 1986
Michael Payne. *Reading Theory: An Introduction to Lacan, Derrida, and Kristeva*, Blackwell, 1993
C. Penley, ed. *Feminism and Film Theory*, Routledge, 1988
—. *et al*, eds. *Close Encounters: Film, Feminism and Science Fiction*, University of Minnesota Press, Minneapolis, 1991
—. & A. Ross, eds. *Technoculture*, University of Minnesota Press, Minneapolis, MN, 1991
Monique Plaza. ""Phallomorphic power" and the psychology of "woman"", *Ideology and Consciousness*, 4, 1978
A. Plotinsky: "The Medusa's Ears: The Question of Nietzsche, the Question of Gender, and Transformation of Theory", in P. Burgard
R. Polt. *Heidegger: An Introduction*, Cornell University Press, 1999
Donald Prater. *A Ringing Glass: The Life of Rainer Maria Rilke*, Clarendon Press, 1994
A. Press. *Women Watching Television*, University of Pennsylvania Press, Philadelphia, 1991
E.D. Pribram, ed. *Female Spectators: Looking At Film and TV*, Verso, 1988
E. Probyn. "Bodies and Anti-bodies" Feminism and the Postmodern", *Cultural Studies*, 1, 3, 1987
—. *Sexing the Self: Gendered Positions in Cultural Studies*, Routledge, N.Y.,

1993

S. Projansky. *Watching Rape: Film and Television in Postfeminism Culture,* New York University Press, 2001

Leslie Rabine. "Écriture Féminine as Metaphor", *Cultural Critique,* 8, Winter, 1987/8

Jean Radford. "Coming to terms: Dorothy Richardson, Modernism and Women", *News From Nowhere,* 7, Winter, 1989

H. Radner. *Shopping Around: Feminine Culture and the Pursuit of Pleasure,* Routledge, N.Y., 1995

H.L. Radtke & H.J. Stam, eds. *Gender and Power,* Sage 1994

Janice Radway. *Reading the Romance: Feminism and the Representation of Women in Popular Culture,* University of North Carolina Press, Chapel Hill, 1984

J.L. Reich. "Genderfuck: The Law of the Dildo", *Discourse: Journal of Theoretical Studies in Media and Culture,* 15, 1, 1992

J. Reinelt & J. Roach, eds. *Critical Theory and Performance,* University of Michigan Press, Ann Arbor, 1992

Philip Rice & Patricia Waugh, eds. *Modern Literary Theory: A Reader,* Arnold, 1992

Adrienne Rich. *Of Woman Born: Motherhood as Experience and Institution,* Virago, 1977

—. *Blood, Bread and Poetry,* Virago, 1980

Michèle Richman. "Sex and Signs: The Language of French Feminist Criticism", *Language and Style,* 13, 4, Autumn, 1980

Rainer Maria Rilke. *The Selected Poetry of Rainer Maria Rilke,* tr. S. Mitchell, Picador, London, 1987

—. *Sonnets to Orpheus,* tr. L. Norris & A. Keele, Skoob Books, London, 1991

Arthur Rimbaud. *Complete Works, Selected Letters,* tr. Wallace Fowlie, University of Chicago Press, Chicago, 1966

Jeanne Addison Roberts. *The Shakespearean Wild: Geography, Genus and Gender,* University of Nebraska Press, Lincoln, Nebraska, 1991

Jacqueline Rose. *Sexuality in the Field of Vision,* Verso, 1986

Françoise van Rossum-Guyon & Myriam Diaz-Diocaretz, eds. *Hélène Cixous: chemins d'une écriture,* Rodopi, Amsterdam, 1990

Tilde Sankovitch. *French Women Writers and the Book: Myths of Access and Desire,* Syracuse University Press, Syracuse, 1988

Eva Martin Sartori & Dorothy Wynne Zimmerman, eds. *French Women Writers,* University Press, Lincoln, 1994

Janet Sayers. *Biological Politics,* Tavistock 1982

John Schad. *Victorians in Theory From Derrida to Browning,* Manchester University Press, 1999

Naomi Schor. *Breaking the Chain: Women, Theory and French Realist Fiction,* New York, 1985
—. & Elizabeth Weed, eds. *Differences: More Gender Trouble: Feminism Meets Queer Theory,* Indiana University Press, 6, 2-3, Summer, 1994
Alan D. Schrift: "On the Gynecology of Morals: Nietzsche and Cixous on the Logic of the Gift", P. Burgard
Thomas A. Sebeok, ed. *The Tell-Tale Sign: A survey of semiotics,* Peter de Ridder Press, Lisse, Netherlands 1975
E. Sedgwick. *Between Men: English Literature and Male Homosexual Desire,* Columbia University Press, N.Y., 1985
—. *Epistemology of the Closet,* Harvester Wheatsheaf, 1991
—. *Tendencies,* Routledge, 1992
Susan Sellers, ed. *Writing Differences: Readings From the Seminar of Hélène Cixous,* Open University Press, 1988
—. ed. *Delighting the Heart: A Notebook by Women Writers,* Women's Press, 1989
—. *Language and Sexual Difference: Feminist Writing in France,* Macmillan, 1991
—. ed. *Feminist Criticism: Theory and Practice,* Harvester Wheatsheaf, 1991
L. Senelick, ed. *Gender in Performance: The Presentation of Difference in the Performing Arts,* University of New England Press, Hanover, 1992
E. Sewell. *The Orphic Voice: Poetry and Natural History,* Routledge, London, 1961
Sheba Collective, eds. *Serious Pleasure: Lesbian Erotic Stories and Poetry,* Cleris, Pittsburgh, 1991
M. Sheiner, ed. *Heroitica 4: A New Collection of Erotic Writing By Women,* Plume, N.Y., 1996
Morag Shiach. *Hélène Cixous: A Politics of Writing,* Routledge, 1991
Elaine Showalter, ed. *The New Feminist Criticism,* Virago, 1986
Kaja Silverman. *The Acoustic Mirror: The Female Voice in Psychoanalysis and Cinema,* Indiana University Press, Bloomington, 1988
C. Sinclair. *Net Chick: A Small Girl Guide to the Wired World,* Henry Holt, N.Y., 1996
M. Slung, ed. *Slow Hand: Women Writing Erotica,* HarperCollins, N.Y., 1992
J. Smith & C. Ferstman. *The Castration of Oedipus: Feminism, Psychoanalysis and the Will to Power,* New York University Press, 1996
C.H. Sommers. *Who Stole Feminism? How Women Have Betrayed Women,* Simon & Schuster, N.Y., 1994
Dale Spender. *The Writing or the Sex? why you don't have to read women's writing to know it's no good,* Pergamon Press, New York, 1989

Gayatri Chakravorty Spivak. "French feminism in an international frame", *Yale French Studies*, 62, 1981
—. *The Post-Colonial Critic: Interviews, Strategies, Dialogues*, ed. Sarah Harasym, Routledge, 1990
George Stambolian & Elaine Marks, eds. *Homosexuality and French Literature: Cultural Contexts/ Critical Texts*, Cornell University Press, Ithaca, 1979
Donna C. Stanton. "Difference on Trial: Critique of the Maternal Metaphor in Cixous, Irigaray, and Kristeva", in N. Miller, 1986
Crista Stevens. "Hélène Cixous: Portraying the Feminine", in L. Brouwer, 1990
H. Stevens & C. Howlett, eds. *Modernist Sexualities*, Manchester University Press, 2000
Judith Still & Michael Worton, eds. *Textuality and Sexuality: Reading Theories and Practices*, Manchester University Press, 1993
John Storey, ed. *Cultural Theory and Popular Culture*, Harvester Wheatsheaf, 1994
N. Strossen. *Defending Pornography: Free Speech, Sex, and the Fight For Women's Rights*, New York University Press, 2000
Susan Rubin Suleiman, ed. *Subversive Intent: Gender, Politics and the Avant-Garde*, Harvard University Press, 1990
—. *Risking Who One Is*, MIT Press, 1995
T. Taormino, ed. *The Best Lesbian Erotica*, Cleis, San Francisco, 1997
L. Thornton *et al*, eds. *Touching Fire: Erotic Writings By Women*, Carroll & Graf, N.Y., 1989
C.S. Vance, ed. *Pleasure and Danger: Exploring Female Sexuality*, Pandora, 1989
S. Walters. *Material Girls: Making Sense of Feminist Cultural Theory*, University of California Press, Berkeley, 1995
Marina Warner: *Monuments and Maidens*, Weidenfeld & Nicholson, 1985
Chris Weedon, *Feminist Practice and Poststructuralist Theory*, Blackwell, 1987
Helene Wenzel. "The text and body/ politics: an appreciation of Monique Wittig's writings in context", *Feminist Studies*, 7, 1981
Margaret Whitford: "Luce Irigaray and the Female Imaginary: Speaking as a Woman", *Radical Philosophy*, 43, 1986
—. "Luce Irigaray", *Paragraph: The Journal of the Modern Critical Theory Group*, 8, October, 1986
—. "Luce Irigaray's Critique of Rationality", in M. Griffiths, 1988
—. *Luce Irigaray: Philosophy in the Feminine*, Routledge, 1991
Helen Wilcox *et al*, eds. *The Body and the Text: Hélène Cixous, Reading and Teaching*, Harvester Wheatsheaf, 1990

S. Wilkinson & C. Kitzinger, eds. *Heterosexuality: A Feminism and Psychology* Reader, Sage, 1993

Linda Ruth Williams. *Critical Desire: Psychoanalysis and the Literary Subject*, Arnold, 1995

—. *Sex in the Head,* Harvester Wheatsheaf, 1995

Sharon Willis. "Mistranslation: *Vivre l'orange*", *SubStance*, 16, 1987

—. "Hélène Cixous's *Portrait de Dora*: The Unseen and the Un-Scene", *Theater Journal,* 37, 1985

Monique Wittig: *Les Guerillères,* tr. David Le Vay, Viking, New York 1971

—. "One is Not Born A Woman", *Feminist Issues*, 1, 3, Winter 1981

—. "Mark of Gender", *Feminist Issues*, 5, 2, 1985

—. *The Lesbian Body*, tr. David Le Vay, Beacon Press, Boston 1986

—. *The Straight Mind,* Beacon Press, Boston 1992

E.V. Wolfenstein. *Inside/ Outside Nietzsche,* Cornell University Press, 2000

J. Wolmark, ed. *Cybersexualities: A Reader on Feminist Theory, Cyborgs and Cyberspace,* Edinburgh University Press, 1999

T. Woods. *Beginning Postmodernism,* Manchester University Press, 1999

Elizabeth Wright, ed. *Feminism and Psychoanalysis: A Critical Dictionary,* Blackwell, 1992

Peter Zima, ed. *Semiotics and Dialectics: Ideology and the Text,* Benjamins, Amsterdam, 1981

Jack Zipes. *Don't Bet On the Prince: Contemporary Feminist Fairy Tales in North America and England*, Methuen, New York, 1986

WEBSITES

irigaray.org
kristeva.fr
kristevacircle.org

CRESCENT MOON PUBLISHING

ARTS, PAINTING, SCULPTURE

The Art of Andy Goldsworthy
Andy Goldsworthy: Touching Nature
Andy Goldsworthy in Close-Up
Andy Goldsworthy: Pocket Guide
Andy Goldsworthy In America

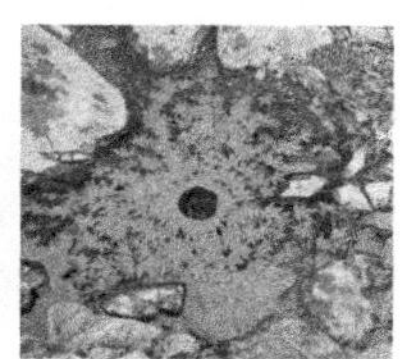

Land Art: A Complete Guide
The Art of Richard Long
Richard Long: Pocket Guide
Land Art In the UK
Land Art in Close-Up
Land Art In the U.S.A.
Land Art: Pocket Guide
Installation Art in Close-Up

Minimal Art and Artists In the 1960s and After
Colourfield Painting
Land Art DVD, TV documentary

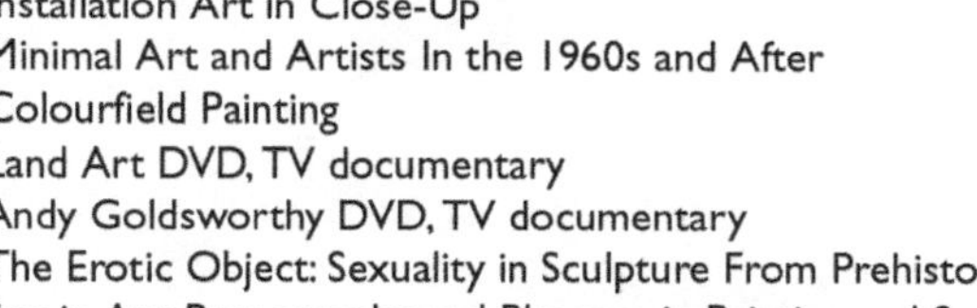

Andy Goldsworthy DVD, TV documentary
The Erotic Object: Sexuality in Sculpture From Prehistory to the Present Day
Sex in Art: Pornography and Pleasure in Painting and Sculpture
Postwar Art
Sacred Gardens: The Garden in Myth, Religion and Art

Glorification: Religious Abstraction in Renaissance and 20th Century Art
Early Netherlandish Painting
Leonardo da Vinci
Piero della Francesca
Giovanni Bellini
Fra Angelico: Art and Religion in the Renaissance
Mark Rothko: The Art of Transcendence
Frank Stella: American Abstract Artist

Jasper Johns
Brice Marden
Alison Wilding: The Embrace of Sculpture
Vincent van Gogh: Visionary Landscapes
Eric Gill: Nuptials of God
Constantin Brancusi: Sculpting the Essence of Things
Max Beckmann
Caravaggio
Gustave Moreau
Egon Schiele: Sex and Death In Purple Stockings
Delizioso Fotografico Fervore: Works In Process 1

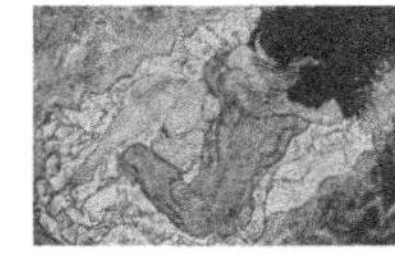

Sacro Cuore: Works In Process 2
The Light Eternal: J.M.W. Turner
The Madonna Glorified: Karen Arthurs

LITERATURE

J.R.R. Tolkien: The Books, The Films, The Whole Cultural Phenomenon
J.R.R. Tolkien: Pocket Guide
Tolkien's Heroic Quest
The *Earthsea* Books of Ursula Le Guin
Beauties, Beasts and Enchantment: Classic French Fairy Tales
German Popular Stories by the Brothers Grimm
Philip Pullman and *His Dark Materials*
Sexing Hardy: Thomas Hardy and Feminism
Thomas Hardy's *Tess of the d'Urbervilles*
Thomas Hardy's *Jude the Obscure*
Thomas Hardy: The Tragic Novels
Love and Tragedy: Thomas Hardy
The Poetry of Landscape in Hardy
Wessex Revisited: Thomas Hardy and John Cowper Powys
Wolfgang Iser: Essays and Interviews
Petrarch, Dante and the Troubadours
Maurice Sendak and the Art of Children's Book Illustration
Andrea Dworkin
Cixous, Irigaray, Kristeva: The *Jouissance* of French Feminism
Julia Kristeva: Art, Love, Melancholy, Philosophy, Semiotics and Psychoanalysis
Hélene Cixous I Love You: The *Jouissance* of Writing
Luce Irigaray: Lips, Kissing, and the Politics of Sexual Difference
Peter Redgrove: Here Comes the Flood
Peter Redgrove: Sex-Magic-Poetry-Cornwall
Lawrence Durrell: Between Love and Death, East and West
Love, Culture & Poetry: Lawrence Durrell
Cavafy: Anatomy of a Soul
German Romantic Poetry: Goethe, Novalis, Heine, Hölderlin
Feminism and Shakespeare
Shakespeare: Love, Poetry & Magic
The Passion of D.H. Lawrence
D.H. Lawrence: Symbolic Landscapes
D.H. Lawrence: Infinite Sensual Violence
Rimbaud: Arthur Rimbaud and the Magic of Poetry
The Ecstasies of John Cowper Powys
Sensualism and Mythology: The Wessex Novels of John Cowper Powys
Amorous Life: John Cowper Powys and the Manifestation of Affectivity (H.W. Fawkner)
Postmodern Powys: New Essays on John Cowper Powys (Joe Boulter)
Rethinking Powys: Critical Essays on John Cowper Powys
Paul Bowles & Bernardo Bertolucci
Rainer Maria Rilke
Joseph Conrad: *Heart of Darkness*
In the Dim Void: Samuel Beckett
Samuel Beckett Goes into the Silence
André Gide: Fiction and Fervour
Jackie Collins and the Blockbuster Novel
Blinded By Her Light: The Love-Poetry of Robert Graves
The Passion of Colours: Travels In Mediterranean Lands
Poetic Forms

POETRY

Ursula Le Guin: Walking In Cornwall
Peter Redgrove: Here Comes The Flood
Peter Redgrove: Sex-Magic-Poetry-Cornwall

Dante: Selections From the Vita Nuova
Petrarch, Dante and the Troubadours
William Shakespeare: Sonnets
William Shakespeare: Complete Poems

Blinded By Her Light: The Love-Poetry of Robert Graves
Emily Dickinson: Selected Poems
Emily Brontë: Poems
Thomas Hardy: Selected Poems
Percy Bysshe Shelley: Poems

John Keats: Selected Poems
Joh n Keats: Poems of 1820
D.H. Lawrence: Selected Poems

Edmund Spenser: Poems
Edmund Spenser: Amoretti
John Donne: Poems

Henry Vaughan: Poems
Sir Thomas Wyatt: Poems
Robert Herrick: Selected Poems
Rilke: Space, Essence and Angels in the Poetry of Rainer Maria Rilke
Rainer Maria Rilke: Selected Poems
Friedrich Hölderlin: Selected Poems
Arseny Tarkovsky: Selected Poems

Arthur Rimbaud: Selected Poems
Arthur Rimbaud: A Season in Hell
Arthur Rimbaud and the Magic of Poetry
Novalis: Hymns To the Night
German Romantic Poetry
Paul Verlaine: Selected Poems
Elizaethan Sonnet Cycles

D.J. Enright: By-Blows
Jeremy Reed: Brigitte's Blue Heart
Jeremy Reed: Claudia Schiffer's Red Shoes
Gorgeous Little Orpheus
Radiance: New Poems
Crescent Moon Book of Nature Poetry
Crescent Moon Book of Love Poetry
Crescent Moon Book of Mystical Poetry
Crescent Moon Book of Elizabethan Love Poetry
Crescent Moon Book of Metaphysical Poetry
Crescent Moon Book of Romantic Poetry
Pagan America: New American Poetry

MEDIA, CINEMA, FEMINISM and CULTURAL STUDIES

J.R.R. Tolkien: The Books, The Films, The Whole Cultural Phenomenon
J.R.R. Tolkien: Pocket Guide
The *Lord of the Rings* Movies: Pocket Guide
The Cinema of Hayao Miyazaki
Hayao Miyazaki: *Princess Mononoke*: Pocket Movie Guide
Hayao Miyazaki: *Spirited Away*: Pocket Movie Guide
Tim Burton
Ken Russell
Ken Russell: *Tommy*: Pocket Movie Guide
The Ghost Dance: The Origins of Religion
The Peyote Cult

Cixous, Irigaray, Kristeva: The *Jouissance* of French Feminism
Julia Kristeva: Art, Love, Melancholy, Philosophy, Semiotics and Psychoanalysis
Luce Irigaray: Lips, Kissing, and the Politics of Sexual Difference
Hélene Cixous I Love You: The *Jouissance* of Writing

Andrea Dworkin
'Cosmo Woman': The World of Women's Magazines
Women in Pop Music
Discovering the Goddess (Geoffrey Ashe)
The Poetry of Cinema

The Sacred Cinema of Andrei Tarkovsky
Andrei Tarkovsky: Pocket Guide
Andrei Tarkovsky: *Mirror*: Pocket Movie Guide
Andrei Tarkovsky: *The Sacrifice*: Pocket Movie Guide
Walerian Borowczyk: Cinema of Erotic Dreams

Jean-Luc Godard: The Passion of Cinema
Jean-Luc Godard: *Hail Mary*: Pocket Movie Guide
Jean-Luc Godard: *Contempt*: Pocket Movie Guide
Jean-Luc Godard: *Pierrot le Fou*: Pocket Movie Guide
John Hughes and Eighties Cinema
Ferris Bueller's Day Off: Pocket Movie Guide

Jean-Luc Godard: Pocket Guide
The Cinema of Richard Linklater
Liv Tyler: Star In Ascendance
Blade Runner and the Films of Philip K. Dick
Paul Bowles and Bernardo Bertolucci
Media Hell: Radio, TV and the Press
An Open Letter to the BBC
Detonation Britain: Nuclear War in the UK

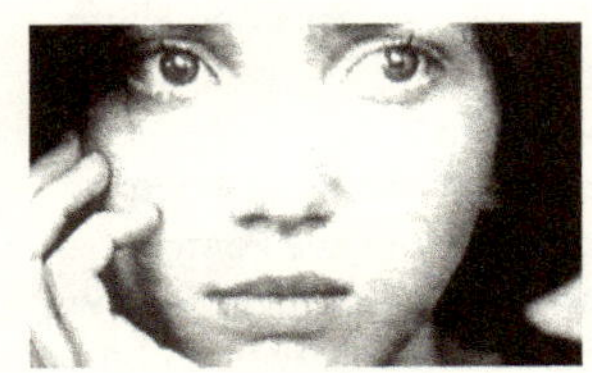

Feminism and Shakespeare
Wild Zones: Pornography, Art and Feminism
Sex in Art: Pornography and Pleasure in Painting and Sculpture
Sexing Hardy: Thomas Hardy and Feminism

In my view *The Light Eternal* is among the very best of all the material I read on Turner. (Douglas Graham, director of the Turner Museum, Denver, Colorado)

The Light Eternal is a model monograph, an exemplary job. The subject matter of the book is beautifully organised and dead on beam. (Lawrence Durrell)

It is amazing for me to see my work treated with such passion and respect. (Andrea Dworkin)

CRESCENT MOON PUBLISHING
P.O. Box 1312, Maidstone, Kent, ME14 5XU, Great Britain. www.crmoon.com

www.ingramcontent.com/pod-product-compliance
Lightning Source LLC
Chambersburg PA
CBHW030835090426
42737CB00009B/976

* 9 7 8 1 8 6 1 7 1 4 1 9 0 *